SUT

D0654223

MATHS ON TARGET

Year 3

Stephen Pearce

Elmwood Press

First published 2008 by
Elmwood Press
80 Attimore Road
Welwyn Garden City
Herts. AL8 6LP
Tel. 01707 333232

Reprinted in 2009

All rights reserved. No part of this publication may be reproduced, stored in a retrieval
system, or transmitted, in any form or by any means, electronic, mechanical,
photocopying, recording or otherwise, without permission in writing from the
publisher or under licence from the Copyright Licensing Agency, Saffron House,
6–10 Kirby Street, London EC1N 8TS.

Any person who commits any unauthorised act in relation to this publication may be
liable to criminal prosecution and civil claims for damages.

© Stephen Pearce
The moral rights of the authors have been asserted.
Database right Elmwood Press (maker)

ISBN 9781 902 214 917

Numerical answers are published in a separate book.

LONDON BOROUGH OF SUTTON LIBRARY SERVICE (SUT)	
30119 028 029 77 7	
Askews & Holts	Jan-2017
J510	

Typeset and illustrated by Tech-Set Ltd., Gateshead, Tyne and Wear.
Printed and bound in Spain on behalf of JFDi Print Services Ltd.

PREFACE

Maths on Target has been written for pupils in Year 3 and their teachers.

The intention of the book is to provide teachers with material to teach all the objectives as set out in the yearly programme in the renewed Primary Framework for Mathematics.

The structure of **Maths on Target** matches that of the renewed framework. It is arranged in five blocks, A–E, each of which consists of three units. To ensure progression throughout the year the units are best taught in the order in which they appear in both this book and the exemplar planning structure for Year 3 in the renewed framework.

	Block A	Block B	Block C	Block D	Block E
Term 1	Unit 1	Unit 1	Unit 1	Unit 1	Unit 1
Term 2	Unit 2	Unit 2	Unit 2	Unit 2	Unit 2
Term 3	Unit 3	Unit 3	Unit 3	Unit 3	Unit 3

Each unit in **Maths on Target** consists of lessons based upon the learning overview for that unit in the renewed framework. Each lesson is divided into four sections:

Introduction: the learning intention expressed as an 'I can' statement and, where necessary, clearly worked examples.

Section A: activities based upon work previously covered. This generally matches the objectives for Year 2 pupils. This section can be used to remind children of work previously covered, as well as providing material for the less confident child.

Section B: activities based upon the objectives for Year 3 pupils. Most children should be able to work successfully at this level.

Section C: activities providing extension material for the faster workers and for those who need to be moved quickly onto more challenging tasks. The work in this section generally matches the objectives for Year 4 pupils. Problems in Section C can also provide useful material for discussion in the plenary session.

The correspondence of the three sections A–C to the objectives for different year groups provides a simple, manageable structure for planning differentiated activities and for both the formal and informal assessment of children's progress. The commonality of the content pitched at different levels also allows for progression within the lesson. Children acquiring confidence at one level find they can successfully complete activities at the next level.

The author is indebted to many colleagues who have assisted him in this work. He is particularly grateful to Sharon Granville and Debra Turner for their invaluable advice and assistance.

Stephen Pearce

CONTENTS

I can read and write whole numbers.

You will need to know and use these words:

1 one	9 nine	17 seventeen	60 sixty
2 two	10 ten	18 eighteen	70 seventy
3 three	11 eleven	19 nineteen	80 eighty
4 four	12 twelve	20 twenty	90 ninety
5 five	13 thirteen	21 twenty-one	100 hundred
6 six	14 fourteen	30 thirty	1000 thousand
7 seven	15 fifteen	40 forty	
8 eight	16 sixteen	50 fifty	

The way we read a digit depends upon its position in the number.

Examples

27 reads *twenty-seven*

274 reads *two hundred and seventy-four*

2745 reads *two thousand seven hundred and forty-five*

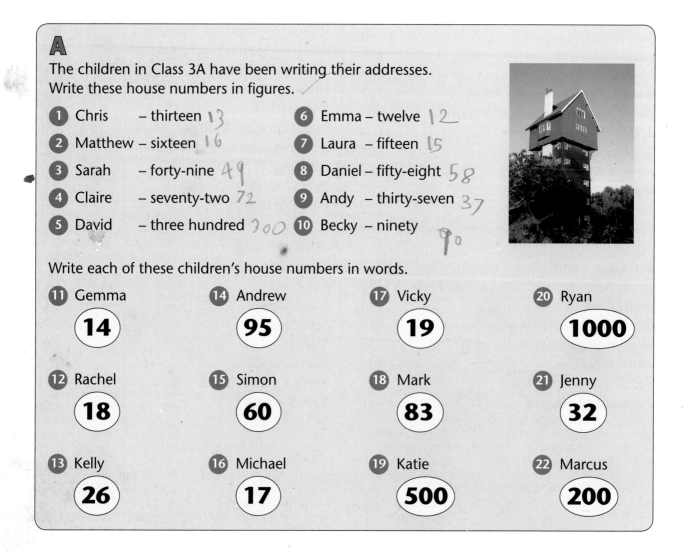

A

The children in Class 3A have been writing their addresses.
Write these house numbers in figures.

1 Chris – thirteen 13

2 Matthew – sixteen 16

3 Sarah – forty-nine 49

4 Claire – seventy-two 72

5 David – three hundred 300

6 Emma – twelve 12

7 Laura – fifteen 15

8 Daniel – fifty-eight 58

9 Andy – thirty-seven 37

10 Becky – ninety 90

Write each of these children's house numbers in words.

11 Gemma **14**

12 Rachel **18**

13 Kelly **26**

14 Andrew **95**

15 Simon **60**

16 Michael **17**

17 Vicky **19**

18 Mark **83**

19 Katie **500**

20 Ryan **1000**

21 Jenny **32**

22 Marcus **200**

B

Write the numbers of these raffle tickets in words.

1. 43 4. 52 7. 424 10. 861
2. 789 5. 238 8. 635 11. 103
3. 176 6. 540 9. 317 12. 908

The prize winning numbers were called out. Draw the tickets.

13. Sixty-five.
14. One hundred and forty-two.
15. Five hundred and ninety-four.
16. Four hundred and sixty.
17. Seventy-seven.
18. Three hundred and five.
19. Two hundred and fifty-one.
20. Eight hundred and twelve.
21. Six hundred and nine.
22. One hundred and eighty.
23. Nine hundred and eighty-four.
24. Seven hundred and seven.

C

Write the heights of these mountains in words.

1. Everest 8848 m
2. Ben Nevis 1343 m
3. Scafell 978 m
4. Elbrus 5033 m
5. Etna 3340 m
6. Mt. McKinley 6195 m
7. Snowdon 1085 m
8. Mont Blanc 4807 m
9. Kilimanjaro 5895 m
10. Annapurna 8078 m

11. Use these digits.

3 1 7 0

Make as many four-digit numbers as you can with a value of less than 2000. There are six. Can you find them all?

Write the numbers:
a) in figures b) in words.

12. Write these numbers in words.
a) 2003 b) 2030 c) 2300 d) 2303 e) 2330

I can identify the position of numbers on a number line and I can use ordinal numbers.

A

What are the two numbers shown on each number line?

1 20 ↓   ↓ 30

2 90 ↓ ↓100

3 0 ↓   ↓ 100

Starting with Sunday, write down which day of the week is:

4 second

5 fifth

6 last

7 third

8 sixth.

Which letter of the alphabet is:

9 first

10 fourth

11 tenth

12 last?

13 What is the fifth number in the two times table?

B

What are the two numbers shown on each number line?

1 250 ↓ ↓ 260

2 300 ↓ ↓ 400

3 0   ↓   ↓1000

Which month of the year is:

4 first

5 eighth

6 last

7 third

8 tenth?

What position in the alphabet is:

9 C

10 M

11 Y

12 T

13 Write down the seventh number in the five times table.

C

What are the two numbers shown on each number line?

1 7000 ↓   ↓ 8000

2 6940 ↓ ↓   6950

3 1100 ↓ ↓ 1200

Here are some red and yellow beads.

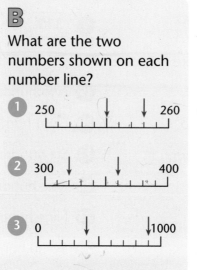

If the pattern was continued, what colour would these beads be?

4 the 15th

5 the 19th

6 the 28th

7 the 32nd

8 the 60th

9 What is the 35th odd number?

10 What is the position of 36 in:

   a) the 4 times table

   b) the 6 times table?

I can count on and back from any given number.

Examples

Count back six steps of 4 from 27.

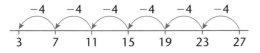

Answer   *3*

Count on six steps of 20 from 15.

```
    +20  +20  +20  +20  +20  +20
  15   35   55   75   95  115  135
```

Answer   *135*

A

Write the first six numbers in each sequence.

1 Start at 16.
   Count on in 2s.

2 Start at 35.
   Count back in 5s.

3 Start at 17.
   Count on in 1s.

4 Start at 24.
   Count back in 4s.

5 Start at 5.
   Count on in 3s.

6 Start at 80.
   Count back in 10s.

7 Start at 7.
   Count on in 4s.

8 Start at 44.
   Count back in 1s.

9 Start at 23.
   Count on in 10s.

10 Start at 30.
   Count back in 3s.

B

Write the next three numbers in each sequence.

1 20   40   60   80

2 150   250   350   450

3 0   6   12   18

4 10   40   70   100

5 20   60   100   140

6 110   160   210   260

7 38   32   26   20

8 200   170   140   110

9 470   420   370   320

10 190   170   150   130

11 600   540   480   420

12 999   899   799   699

What is the smallest number I get if I count back:

13 in 5s from 37

14 in 4s from 23

15 in 6s from 43

16 in 20s from 91?

C

Write the next three numbers in each sequence.

1 14   22   30   38

2 200   175   150   125

3 0   7   14   21

4 86   75   64   53

5 76   67   58   49

6 0   15   30   45

7 100   300   500   700

8 100   88   76   64

What number did I start from?

9 I count back five 50s and I am left with 28.

10 I count back three 100s and I am left with 17.

11 I count back six 7s and I am left with 5.

12 I count back four 9s and I am left with 3.

I can count in groups of 2, 5, 10 and 20.

A

1. How many groups of 2 make three groups of 4?

2. How many groups of 4 make eight groups of 2?

3. How many groups of 5 make four groups of 10?

4. How many groups of 10 make four groups of 5?

Count up in groups.

5.

6.

7.

Use 20 counters.

8. How many groups of 10?

9. How many groups of 5?

10. How many groups of 2?

11. How many groups of 4?

12. How many groups of ten make 60?

13. How many groups of 5 make 35?

14. How many groups of 2 make 18?

B

1. How many groups of 6 make four groups of 3?

2. How many groups of 3 make five groups of 6?

3. How many groups of 10 make three groups of 20?

4. How many groups of 20 make eight groups of 10?

How much money?

5. five 2ps

6. seven 10ps

7. nine 5ps

8. five 20ps

Use 38 counters.

9. How many groups of 10?

10. How many groups of 5?

11. How many groups of 4?

12. How many groups of 6?

13. How many groups of 10 make 100?

14. How many groups of 20 make 100?

15. How many groups of 5 make 100?

C

1. How many 5-a-side football teams can be made from a class of 28 children?
How many children are left over?

2. Zoe has three 20ps and three 5ps.
How much does she have altogether?

3. How many wheels are there on eleven bicycles?

4. How many 5ps make one pound?

5. There are 180 children in a school. They sit in rows of 20. How many rows are there?

6. How many days make five weeks?

7. How many boxes of 6 can be filled from 25 eggs?
How many eggs are left over?

8. Four children sit at each table.
How many tables are needed for 28 children?

9. How many 2ps make 50p?

I can partition (split) a number into hundreds, tens and ones.

Examples

369   The 3 has a value of 300.   517   The 5 has a value of 500.
       The 6 has a value of 60.   The 1 has a value of 10.
       The 9 has a value of 9 units.   The 7 has a value of 7 units.

Knowing the value of the digits means that you are able to partition numbers.

Examples

369 = 300 + 60 + 9   517 = 500 + 10 + 7

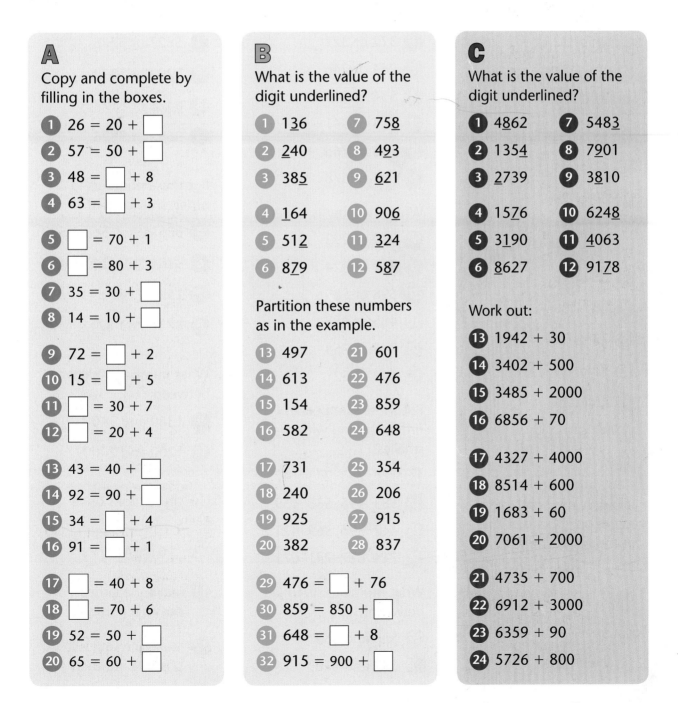

A

Copy and complete by filling in the boxes.

1. 26 = 20 + ☐
2. 57 = 50 + ☐
3. 48 = ☐ + 8
4. 63 = ☐ + 3

5. ☐ = 70 + 1
6. ☐ = 80 + 3
7. 35 = 30 + ☐
8. 14 = 10 + ☐

9. 72 = ☐ + 2
10. 15 = ☐ + 5
11. ☐ = 30 + 7
12. ☐ = 20 + 4

13. 43 = 40 + ☐
14. 92 = 90 + ☐
15. 34 = ☐ + 4
16. 91 = ☐ + 1

17. ☐ = 40 + 8
18. ☐ = 70 + 6
19. 52 = 50 + ☐
20. 65 = 60 + ☐

B

What is the value of the digit underlined?

1. 1<u>3</u>6
2. <u>2</u>40
3. 38<u>5</u>
4. <u>1</u>64
5. 51<u>2</u>
6. 8<u>7</u>9
7. 75<u>8</u>
8. 4<u>9</u>3
9. <u>6</u>21
10. 90<u>6</u>
11. <u>3</u>24
12. 5<u>8</u>7

Partition these numbers as in the example.

13. 497
14. 613
15. 154
16. 582
17. 731
18. 240
19. 925
20. 382
21. 601
22. 476
23. 859
24. 648
25. 354
26. 206
27. 915
28. 837

29. 476 = ☐ + 76
30. 859 = 850 + ☐
31. 648 = ☐ + 8
32. 915 = 900 + ☐

C

What is the value of the digit underlined?

1. 4<u>8</u>62
2. 135<u>4</u>
3. <u>2</u>739
4. 15<u>7</u>6
5. 3<u>1</u>90
6. <u>8</u>627
7. 548<u>3</u>
8. 7<u>9</u>01
9. 38<u>1</u>0
10. 624<u>8</u>
11. <u>4</u>063
12. 91<u>7</u>8

Work out:

13. 1942 + 30
14. 3402 + 500
15. 3485 + 2000
16. 6856 + 70
17. 4327 + 4000
18. 8514 + 600
19. 1683 + 60
20. 7061 + 2000
21. 4735 + 700
22. 6912 + 3000
23. 6359 + 90
24. 5726 + 800

I can put numbers to 1000 in order.

Examples

Put these numbers in order with the smallest first.   651 561 647

Look at the hundreds first.   651 561 647

If the hundreds are the same look at the tens.   651 647

The correct order is   561, 647, 651.

A

Which number is smaller?

1. 27 or 72
2. 57 or 75
3. 76 or 67
4. 63 or 36
5. 43 or 34
6. 89 or 98

Which number is larger?

7. 83 or 38
8. 68 or 86
9. 73 or 37
10. 52 or 25
11. 45 or 54
12. 87 or 78

Copy and complete by filling in any numbers in the boxes so that the numbers are in order.

13. ☐ 48 ☐ 50 51
14. ☐ 36 ☐ 42 47
15. 66 67 ☐ ☐ 70
16. 74 ☐ 82 ☐ 90

B

Which number is smaller?

1. 372 or 327
2. 264 or 246
3. 534 or 543
4. 514 or 541
5. 756 or 765
6. 687 or 678

Which number is larger?

7. 239 or 293
8. 342 or 324
9. 598 or 589
10. 485 or 458
11. 745 or 754
12. 612 or 621

Put these numbers in order, starting with the smallest.

13. 174 253 273 147
14. 583 495 538 459
15. 412 396 369 421
16. 714 682 741 671

What multiples of 10 lie between:

17. 526 and 552
18. 392 and 418?

C

Which number is larger?

1. 5827 or 5728
2. 5293 or 5392
3. 6471 or 6174
4. 9682 or 9826

Put these numbers in order, smallest first.

5. 625 5962 568 6529
6. 3784 473 3478 437
7. 1524 2145 541 2514
8. 8731 783 8713 1378

What number is halfway between:

9. 1360 and 1400
10. 1200 and 2000?

Use these digits once each.

3 6 4 7

11. Make the largest possible number.
12. Make the smallest possible number.

I can add or subtract multiples of 10 or 100.

Examples

357 + 1 = 358   357 − 1 = 356   357 + 30
357 + 10 = 367   357 − 10 = 347
357 + 100 = 457   357 − 100 = 257   357 − 200

```
      +10      +10      +10
357      367      377      387

      −100     −100
157      257      357
```

A

Work out

1. 68 + 1
2. 29 + 1
3. 114 − 1
4. 109 − 1

5. 35 + 10
6. 61 + 10
7. 52 − 10
8. 48 − 10

9. 147 + 100
10. 250 + 100
11. 320 − 100
12. 564 − 100

13. Nikki has £189. She spends £100. How much does she have left?

14. There is 75 ml of medicine in a bottle. Lloyd takes two 10 ml spoonfuls. How much medicine is left?

B

Work out

1. 217 + 10
2. 278 + 10
3. 135 − 10
4. 463 − 10

5. 158 + 30
6. 803 + 50
7. 397 − 60
8. 569 − 40

9. 441 + 200
10. 35 + 500
11. 682 − 300
12. 714 − 200

13. Mark weighs 42 kg. His father weighs 30 kg more. How much does Mark's father weigh?

14. Mr. Patel drives 200 km through France. He works out that he has 289 km to go. How long is his journey?

C

Work out

1. 1364 + 20
2. 2600 + 30
3. 6755 − 40
4. 3917 − 20

5. 1573 + 300
6. 3958 + 400
7. 4892 − 500
8. 6020 − 200

9. 2011 + 5000
10. 3746 + 3000
11. 2489 − 2000
12. 9065 − 4000

13. A parcel weighs 375 g. A second parcel weighs 400 g. How much do the parcels weigh altogether?

14. Kim has £5825 in her bank account. On Monday she pays in £300. On Tuesday she takes out £50. How much does she now have in her account?

I can locate multiples of 10 or 100 on a number line.

A

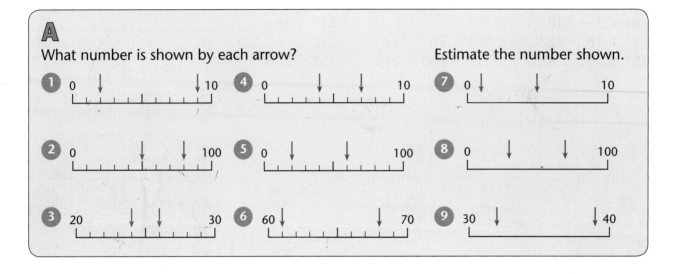

What number is shown by each arrow?   Estimate the number shown.

1. 0 ———— 10
4. 0 ———— 10
7. 0 ———— 10

2. 0 ———— 100
5. 0 ———— 100
8. 0 ———— 100

3. 20 ———— 30
6. 60 ———— 70
9. 30 ———— 40

B

What number is shown by each arrow?   Estimate the number shown.

1. 200 ———— 300
4. 900 ———— 1000
7. 700 ———— 800

2. 0 ———— 1000
5. 0 ———— 1000
8. 0 ———— 1000

3. 160 ———— 170
6. 740 ———— 750
9. 310 ———— 320

C

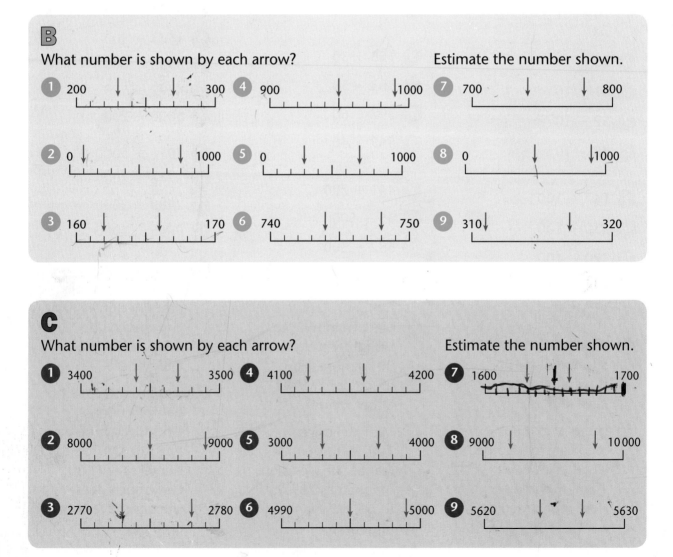

What number is shown by each arrow?   Estimate the number shown.

1. 3400 ———— 3500
4. 4100 ———— 4200
7. 1600 ———— 1700

2. 8000 ———— 9000
5. 3000 ———— 4000
8. 9000 ———— 10 000

3. 2770 ———— 2780
6. 4990 ———— 5000
9. 5620 ———— 5630

I can add or subtract mentally one-digit numbers to or from two-digit numbers.

Examples

COUNTING ON/BACK

36 + 5

| 36 | 37 | 38 | 39 | 40 | 41 |

39 − 5

| 34 | 35 | 36 | 37 | 38 | 39 |

BRIDGING

74 − 6

−2   −4

| 68 | 70 | 74 |

77 + 8

+3   +5

| 77 | 80 | 85 |

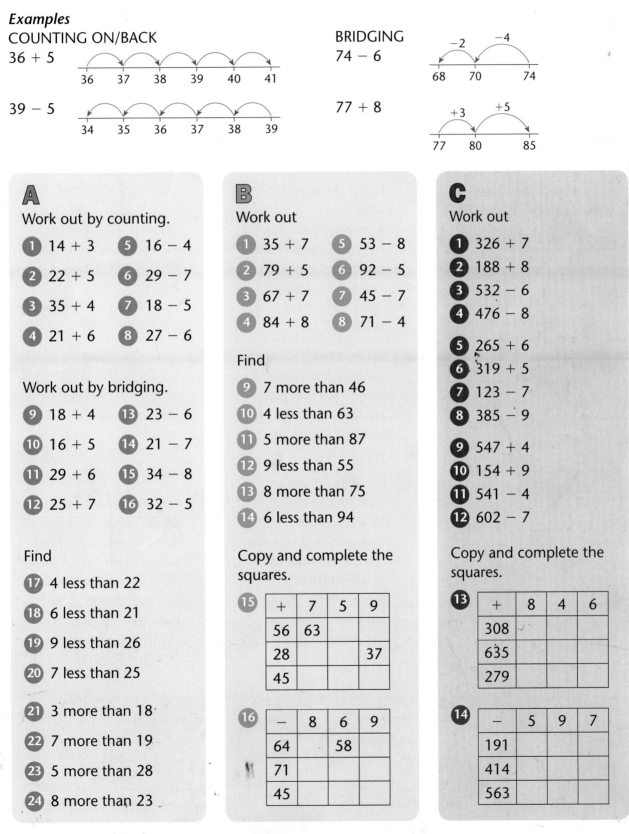

A

Work out by counting.

1. 14 + 3   5. 16 − 4
2. 22 + 5   6. 29 − 7
3. 35 + 4   7. 18 − 5
4. 21 + 6   8. 27 − 6

Work out by bridging.

9. 18 + 4   13. 23 − 6
10. 16 + 5   14. 21 − 7
11. 29 + 6   15. 34 − 8
12. 25 + 7   16. 32 − 5

Find

17. 4 less than 22
18. 6 less than 21
19. 9 less than 26
20. 7 less than 25
21. 3 more than 18
22. 7 more than 19
23. 5 more than 28
24. 8 more than 23

B

Work out

1. 35 + 7   5. 53 − 8
2. 79 + 5   6. 92 − 5
3. 67 + 7   7. 45 − 7
4. 84 + 8   8. 71 − 4

Find

9. 7 more than 46
10. 4 less than 63
11. 5 more than 87
12. 9 less than 55
13. 8 more than 75
14. 6 less than 94

Copy and complete the squares.

15.

+	7	5	9
56	63		
28			37
45			

16.

−	8	6	9
64		58	
71			
45			

C

Work out

1. 326 + 7
2. 188 + 8
3. 532 − 6
4. 476 − 8

5. 265 + 6
6. 319 + 5
7. 123 − 7
8. 385 − 9

9. 547 + 4
10. 154 + 9
11. 541 − 4
12. 602 − 7

Copy and complete the squares.

13.

+	8	4	6
308			
635			
279			

14.

−	5	9	7
191			
414			
563			

I can solve problems and puzzles organising my answers in a systematic way when necessary.

Example

Complete this number sentence in as many ways as possible.

☐6 + 8 = ☐☐

16 + 8 = 24	56 + 8 = 64
26 + 8 = 34	66 + 8 = 74
36 + 8 = 44	76 + 8 = 84
46 + 8 = 54	86 + 8 = 94

Listing the answers in a systematic way makes sure that all the solutions are found.

A

1. Daniel has three 10ps and four 2ps. How much does he have?

2. Lily has five 5ps and three 2ps. How much does she have?

3. Ali has six 10ps and two 5ps. How much does he have?

4. Ella has 2ps and 5ps only. She makes 19p. She uses one 5p. How many 2ps does she use?

5. Will also makes 19p using 2ps and 5ps only. He finds a different way to Ella. How does Will make 19p?

6. Amy puts two 10 g weights and three 5 g weights on a balance. What is the weight on the balance?

Complete each number sentence in as many ways as possible.

7. 15 + ☐ = 2☐

8. 13 − ☐ = ☐

B

1. Alfie, Lucy and Sam buy a drink each for 67p.
   Alfie pays with 5ps.
   Lucy pays with 10ps.
   Sam pays with 20ps.
   How many coins does each child need?

2. James has 85 g on a balance. He takes off three 10 g weights. He takes off four 2 g weights. How much weight is left?

3. Evie has 26 straws. She uses all the straws to make triangles and squares. She finds two ways of doing this so that there are no straws left over. What are the two different ways?

Complete each number sentence in as many ways as possible.

4. ☐6 − 9 = ☐☐

5. 7☐ + ☐7 = ☐☐

C

1. Naseema, Ellie and Mia each buy a sandwich for £1·55.
   Naseema pays with 10ps.
   Ellie pays with 20ps.
   Mia pays with 50ps.
   How many coins does each girl need?

2. Leah has 230 g on a balance. She takes off four 20 g weights. She takes off three 5 g weights. How much weight is left?

3. Cinema tickets cost £5 for adults and £3 for children. Mrs. Prior buys tickets for £43. How many adult tickets has she bought and how many tickets for children? Find all the possible solutions.

Complete each number sentence in as many ways as possible.

4. ☐2 − ☐8 = ☐

5. ☐☐☐ − ☐ = ☐7

I can use addition and subtraction facts for all numbers up to 20.

A

Write the answers only.

1. 4 + 3
5. 7 + 3
2. 7 + 2
6. 5 + 2
3. 6 + 4
7. 3 + 6
4. 5 + 3
8. 2 + 8

9. 8 − 5
13. 10 − 5
10. 10 − 7
14. 9 − 5
11. 9 − 4
15. 8 − 3
12. 10 − 6
16. 10 − 4

17. 40 + 40
21. 50 + 50
18. 20 + 70
22. 30 + 40
19. 60 + 20
23. 40 + 60
20. 30 + 70
24. 60 + 30

25. 100 − 50
26. 90 − 50
27. 80 − 30
28. 100 − 40
29. 70 − 40
30. 100 − 80
31. 90 − 30
32. 80 − 40

33. Copy and complete using the three given numbers only.

8 + 6 = 14

$\square$ + $\square$ = 14

$\square$ − $\square$ = 6

$\square$ − $\square$ = 8

B

Write the answers only.

1. 7 + 8
5. 9 + 7
2. 5 + 8
6. 10 + 8
3. 8 + 9
7. 8 + 6
4. 6 + 6
8. 9 + 9

9. 20 − 8
13. 15 − 8
10. 18 − 11
14. 16 − 9
11. 17 − 8
15. 14 − 6
12. 19 − 12
16. 20 − 13

17. 60 + 90
21. 80 + 80
18. 60 + 80
22. 70 + 70
19. 70 + 90
23. 50 + 70
20. 50 + 90
24. 90 + 80

25. 130 − 50
26. 190 − 70
27. 180 − 90
28. 160 − 70
29. 170 − 60
30. 140 − 80
31. 200 − 90
32. 190 − 140

For each fact write three other facts.

33. 48 + 37 = 85
34. 68 − 35 = 33
35. 53 + 21 = 74
36. 92 − 63 = 29

C

Copy and complete.

1. 60 + $\square$ = 120
2. 70 + $\square$ = 150
3. $\square$ + 60 = 140
4. $\square$ + 70 = 160

5. 200 − $\square$ = 110
6. 150 − $\square$ = 80
7. $\square$ − 90 = 90
8. $\square$ − 70 = 90

9. 80 + $\square$ = 180
10. 80 + $\square$ = 130
11. $\square$ + 90 = 150
12. $\square$ + 80 = 150

13. 190 − $\square$ = 80
14. 180 − $\square$ = 130
15. $\square$ − 70 = 130
16. $\square$ − 80 = 90

Use the three numbers given to write four number facts.

17. 33, 17, 50
18. 52, 28, 24
19. 67, 26, 93
20. 17, 75, 58

I can count on and back from zero in steps of 2, 3, 4, 5, 6 and 10.

A

What is

1. 3×2
2. 7×2
3. 10×2
4. 6×2

5. 4×5
6. 5×5
7. 9×5
8. 8×5

9. 7×10
10. 9×10
11. 2×10
12. 10×10

13. $18 \div 2$
14. $8 \div 2$
15. $16 \div 2$
16. $10 \div 2$

17. $15 \div 5$
18. $30 \div 5$
19. $35 \div 5$
20. $50 \div 5$

21. $40 \div 10$
22. $10 \div 10$
23. $50 \div 10$
24. $80 \div 10$

B

Copy and complete.

1. $\Box \times 2 = 12$
2. $\Box \times 5 = 45$
3. $\Box \times 10 = 70$
4. $\Box \times 2 = 4$

5. $\Box \times 5 = 50$
6. $\Box \times 10 = 10$
7. $\Box \div 2 = 7$
8. $\Box \div 5 = 8$

9. $\Box \div 10 = 4$
10. $\Box \div 2 = 10$
11. $\Box \div 5 = 6$
12. $\Box \div 10 = 9$

Write the answer only.

13. 5×3
14. 9×3
15. 7×3
16. 4×3

17. 10×4
18. 3×4
19. 8×4
20. 6×4

21. 2×6
22. 7×6
23. 4×6
24. 8×6

25. $9 \div 3$
26. $24 \div 3$
27. $18 \div 3$
28. $30 \div 3$

29. $20 \div 4$
30. $36 \div 4$
31. $16 \div 4$
32. $28 \div 4$

33. $36 \div 6$
34. $6 \div 6$
35. $18 \div 6$
36. $54 \div 6$

C

Copy and complete.

1. $\Box \times 3 = 18$
2. $\Box \times 4 = 20$
3. $\Box \times 6 = 36$
4. $\Box \times 3 = 24$

5. $\Box \times 4 = 36$
6. $\Box \times 6 = 30$
7. $\Box \div 3 = 7$
8. $\Box \div 4 = 8$

9. $\Box \div 6 = 4$
10. $\Box \div 3 = 9$
11. $\Box \div 4 = 6$
12. $\Box \div 6 = 7$

Write the answer only.

13. 2×7
14. 7×7
15. 4×7
16. 9×7

17. 10×8
18. 6×8
19. 3×8
20. 8×8

21. 5×9
22. 4×9
23. 9×9
24. 7×9

25. $35 \div 7$
26. $56 \div 7$
27. $42 \div 7$
28. $21 \div 7$

29. $32 \div 8$
30. $16 \div 8$
31. $72 \div 8$
32. $56 \div 8$

33. $9 \div 9$
34. $54 \div 9$
35. $27 \div 9$
36. $72 \div 9$

I can identify numbers to 1000 that are multiples of 2, 5 or 10 and recognise some multiples of 3, 4 and 6.

Multiples are the numbers in a multiplication table.

Examples
The multiples of 2 are 2, 4, 6, 8, 10, 12, and so on
The multiples of 3 are 3, 6, 9, 12, 15, 18, and so on

A

Write the first four multiples of:

1. 2
2. 5
3. 10
4. 3.

Write down the numbers in the ring which are multiples of:

5. 2
6. 5
7. 10.

(15 14 8 100 20 30)

Copy and complete the sentences.

8. The multiples of 2 are ☐ numbers.
9. The multiples of 5 end in ☐ or ☐.
10. The multiples of 10 end in ☐.
11. The multiples of ☐ end in 00.

B

Write the first four multiples of:

1. 4
2. 6
3. 100
4. 50.

Write down the numbers in the ring which are multiples of:

5. 2
6. 5
7. 10.

(201 504 158 700 355 450)

Which number should not be in the box?

8. Multiples of 5
15, 10, 12, 25
9. Multiples of 3
9, 10, 15, 24
10. Multiples of 4
14, 16, 20, 32
11. Multiples of 6
30, 18, 26, 48

C

1. Is 36 a multiple of 4?
2. Is 23 a multiple of 3?
3. Is 16 a multiple of 2?
4. Is 54 a multiple of 6?
5. Is 552 a multiple of 5?
6. Is 205 a multiple of 10?
7. Is 27 a multiple of 3?
8. Is 26 a multiple of 4?
9. Is 42 a multiple of 6?
10. Is 225 a multiple of 2?
11. 10 is a multiple of 2 and a multiple of 5. Find another number that is a multiple of both 2 and 5.
12. Find two numbers that are multiples of both:
    a) 2 and 3
    b) 3 and 4
    c) 3 and 5
    d) 5 and 10
    e) 4 and 5.

I can add and subtract efficiently by bridging, by adding numbers in any order and by identifying pairs of numbers that make 10.

Examples

BRIDGING
67 + 9   54 − 7

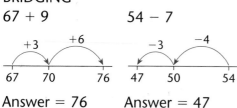

Answer = 76   Answer = 47

STARTING WITH THE
LARGEST NUMBER
7 + 5 + 48

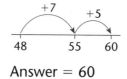

Answer = 60

LOOKING FOR PAIRS
THAT MAKE 10
9 + 2 + 6 + 8 = 10 + 9 + 6
             = 19 + 6
             = 25

A

Work out by bridging.

1 9 + 4   9 15 − 6

2 7 + 5   10 13 − 5

3 6 + 8   11 12 − 4

4 8 + 7   12 17 − 9

5 15 + 6   13 24 − 8

6 17 + 7   14 21 − 4

7 18 + 4   15 26 − 7

8 19 + 6   16 23 − 6

Work out

17 6 + 37   21 9 + 53

18 5 + 29   22 4 + 37

19 8 + 48   23 6 + 48

20 7 + 65   24 7 + 29

Find the totals.

25 3 + 7 + 8

26 2 + 6 + 14

27 9 + 8 + 2

28 4 + 4 + 6

B

Work out by bridging.

1 38 + 6   9 93 − 9

2 65 + 7   10 54 − 6

3 89 + 8   11 47 − 8

4 43 + 9   12 81 − 7

5 76 + 5   13 36 − 9

6 34 + 7   14 62 − 6

7 58 + 9   15 45 − 8

8 67 + 6   16 98 − 9

Copy and complete.

17 4 + 8 + 28 = ☐

18 6 + ☐ + 37 = 51

19 9 + 4 + 24 + ☐ = 40

20 6 + ☐ + 7 + 36 = 54

Copy and complete.

21 5 + 7 + 5 = ☐

22 9 + 4 + ☐ + 6 = 25

23 3 + 8 + ☐ + 7 = 29

24 ☐ + 9 + 6 + 11 = 38

C

Copy and complete.

1 94 + ☐ = 101

2 98 + ☐ = 107

3 97 + ☐ = 102

4 95 + ☐ = 103

5 62 − ☐ = 48

6 85 − ☐ = 63

7 74 + ☐ = 23

8 53 + ☐ = 18

Add up each set of numbers.

9 7, 9, 14, 25

10 16, 5, 8, 43

11 3, 34, 9, 12

12 6, 17, 5, 28

13 9, 3, 8, 36

14 20, 30, 80, 40

15 10, 60, 40, 50

16 50, 30, 40, 70

17 50, 80, 50, 30

18 10, 60, 70, 90

I can use known number facts to find new facts.

Example 1
4 + 8 = 12
40 + 80 = 120
400 + 800 = 1200

Example 2
3 + 7 = 10
30 + 70 = 100
300 + 700 = 1000

Example 3
Double 8 = 16
Double 80 = 160
Double 800 = 1600

A

Copy and complete as in Example 1.

1. 5 + 3 = 8
   50 + ☐ = ☐
   500 + ☐ = ☐

2. 3 + 4 = 7
   ☐ + ☐ = 70
   ☐ + ☐ = 700

3. 6 − 2 = 4
   60 − ☐ = ☐
   600 − ☐ = ☐

4. 9 − 6 = 3
   ☐ − ☐ = 30
   ☐ − ☐ = 300

What needs to be added to each number to make 10?

5. 2
6. 5
7. 8
8. 3
9. 7
10. 4
11. 1
12. 6

Double
13. 4
14. 9
15. 3
16. 6
17. 8
18. 2
19. 7
20. 5

B

Copy and complete.

1. 60 + ☐ = 130
2. 80 + ☐ = 110
3. 40 + ☐ = 130
4. 70 + ☐ = 120
5. 500 + ☐ = 700
6. 200 + ☐ = 500
7. 400 + ☐ = 900
8. 700 + ☐ = 900
9. 110 − ☐ = 40
10. 120 − ☐ = 90
11. 150 − ☐ = 80
12. 130 − ☐ = 50

What needs to be added to each number to make 100?

13. 60
14. 90
15. 30
16. 50
17. 70
18. 40
19. 80
20. 20

Double
21. 20
22. 70
23. 40
24. 90
25. 30
26. 80
27. 60
28. 50

C

Copy and complete.

1. 150 + ☐ = 310
2. 320 + ☐ = 500
3. 270 + ☐ = 530
4. 430 + ☐ = 580
5. 280 − ☐ = 120
6. 670 − ☐ = 340
7. 360 − ☐ = 280
8. 510 − ☐ = 370
9. 100 − ☐ = 45
10. 100 − ☐ = 65
11. 100 − ☐ = 15
12. 100 − ☐ = 75
13. 1000 − ☐ = 350
14. 1000 − ☐ = 50
15. 1000 − ☐ = 550
16. 1000 − ☐ = 850

Double
17. 45
18. 25
19. 65
20. 350
21. 150
22. 750
23. 24
24. 39
25. 58
26. 160
27. 710
28. 950

I can solve one-step and two-step word problems.

Example
There are three eggs in 6 nests and four eggs in 8 nests. How many eggs are there altogether?

$6 \times 3 = 18$
$8 \times 4 = 32$
$18 + 32 = 50$
There are 50 eggs altogether.

A

1. A sack has 43 kg of potatoes. 11 kg of potatoes are used. What is the weight of the potatoes left in the sack?

2. A box of apples weighs 6 kg. How much do 5 boxes weigh?

3. Five people can sit at one table. How many people can sit at seven tables?

4. Donna is 16 years old. Scott is half her age. How old is Scott?

5. A professor has 50 books. He reads 20 in the first month and 15 more in the second month. How many of the books has he not yet read?

6. Isabelle has four 5ps and three 10ps. How much does she have altogether?

B

1. Seven buckets are used to fill a fish tank. Each bucket holds 3 litres. How much water is in the fish tank?

2. A newsagent has 100 newspapers. He sells 68. How many newspapers are left?

3. Darren has 23 marbles. Nathan has 12 more. How many marbles do they have altogether?

4. Jamie buys three packets of 8 Christmas cards and one box of 25 cards. How many cards has he bought?

5. There is one litre of juice in a carton. 400 ml is poured into a jar. The rest is poured equally into three glasses. How much juice is in each glass?

6. Hassan buys two pencils for 19p each. He pays with 50p. How much change is he given?

C

1. Eight children shared 40 sweets equally between them. How many sweets did each child receive?

2. Four classes in a school have 25 children each. The other four classes have 30 children each. How many children are there in the school?

3. A cake weighs 400 g. It is cut into ten equal slices. Three slices are eaten. What is the weight of the cake that is left?

4. Jason has 17 more books on his top shelf than on his bottom shelf. He has 45 books on his top shelf. How many books does Jason have altogether?

5. There are 20 identical books in a pile. The pile is 60 cm high. How thick is each book?

I can use my understanding of number relationships to make up problems and solve puzzles.

Examples

Make up a story match this number sentence.

$$60 - 28 = 32$$

Sarah had 60p. She spent 28p.
She had 32p left.

Find this 2-digit number.
Its digits total 9 and have a difference of 3.

$$3 + 6 = 9 \qquad 6 - 3 = 3$$

Answer   *36 or 63*

A

Make up a story to match each number sentence.

1. $15 + 12 = 27$
2. $24 - 13 = 11$
3. $8 \times 10 = 80$
4. $16 \div 2 = 8$

Give two examples to match each statement.

5. You can add 9 by adding 10 and taking away 1.
6. The order in which you add two numbers does not change the answer.

Find the number.

7. between 20 and 30 the sum of its digits is 7
8. between 12 and 19 a multiple of 5
9. between 30 and 40 the difference between its digits is 4
10. between 25 and 30 a multiple of 4.

B

Make up a story to match each number sentence.

1. $54 + 46 = 100$
2. $40 - 17 = 23$
3. $24 \times 5 = 120$
4. $36 \div 4 = 9$

Give three examples to match each statement.

5. An even number is the sum of two odd numbers.
6. The order in which you multiply two numbers does not change the answer.

Find the number.

7. a 2-digit number its digits have a total of 12 and a difference of 6.
8. a multiple of 9 between 20 and 50 an even number
9. a 2-digit number its digits have a total of 13 and a difference of 3.

C

Make up a story to match each number sentence.

1. $84 - 36 = 48$
2. $30 \times 4 = 120$
3. $64 + 48 = 112$
4. $66 \div 2 = 33$

Give three examples to match each statement.

5. You can add 99 by adding 100 and subtracting 1.
6. Halving and halving again is the same as dividing by 4.

Find a pair of numbers which:

7. multiply to make 6 and have a sum of 5
8. multiply to make 27 and have a sum of 12
9. multiply to make 28 and have a sum of 11
10. multiply to make 120 and have a sum of 22.

I can recognise and describe 3-D shapes.

Names of 3-D shapes with curved faces.
  sphere
  hemi-sphere
  cone
  cylinder

Names of 3-D shapes with straight edges.
  cube
  cuboid
  square based pyramid
  triangular based pyramid

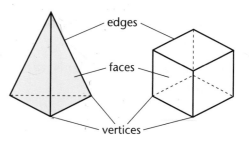

A

Here are some shapes.

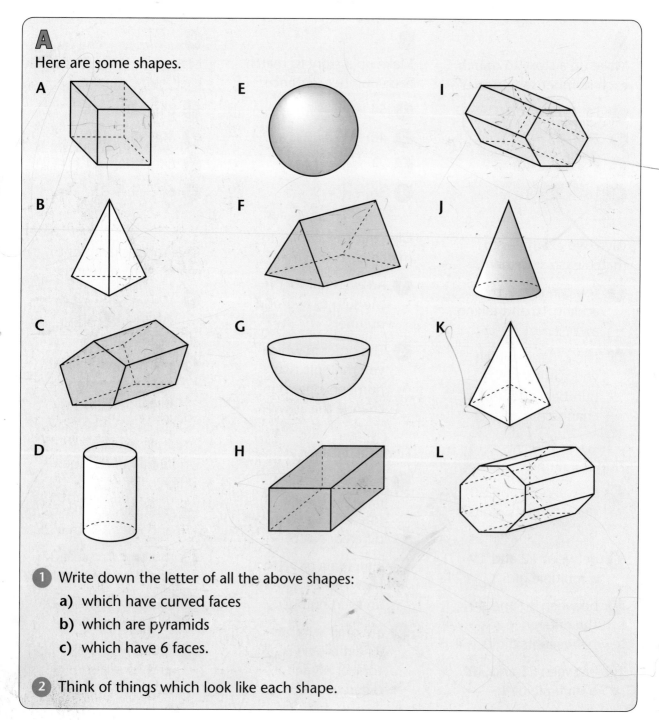

1. Write down the letter of all the above shapes:
   a) which have curved faces
   b) which are pyramids
   c) which have 6 faces.

2. Think of things which look like each shape.

B

A prism is a 3-D shape with two identical end faces and the same cross section throughout its length.

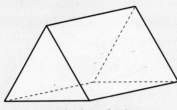

triangular based prism

Look at the shapes on page 20.

1 Give the letter of:

a) the triangular based prism

b) the hexagonal based prism

c) the pentagonal based prism

d) the octagonal (8 sides) based prism.

2 Which two other shapes are also prisms?

3 How many edges are there in:

a) a triangular based prism

b) a pentagonal based prism?

4 Are the number of edges of a prism always a multiple of 3? Give three examples.

Look at the shapes on page 20.
Give the name and letter of a shape with:

5 square faces only

6 15 edges

7 no edges

8 6 rectangular faces

9 6 vertices

10 2 flat faces and 1 curved face

11 5 faces and 8 edges

12 8 faces.

C

Name the odd one out in each group.
Give a reason for your choice.

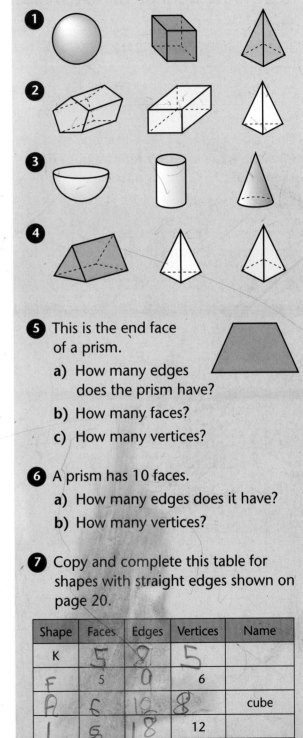

5 This is the end face of a prism.

a) How many edges does the prism have?

b) How many faces?

c) How many vertices?

6 A prism has 10 faces.

a) How many edges does it have?

b) How many vertices?

7 Copy and complete this table for shapes with straight edges shown on page 20.

Shape	Faces	Edges	Vertices	Name
K	5	8	5	
F	5	0	6	
A	6	12	8	cube
I	5	18	12	
B	4	6	4	
C	7	15	10	
H	6	12	8	
	10	24	16	

I can choose a shape to match given properties and make and draw 2-D shapes.

CURVED SHAPES

A circle and a semi-circle have curved edges.

TRIANGLES

A 2-D shape with three straight edges is a triangle.

QUADRILATERALS

A 2-D shape with four straight edges is a quadrilateral. Squares are quadrilaterals.

POLYGONS

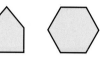

5 sides – pentagon
6 sides – hexagon
8 sides – octagon

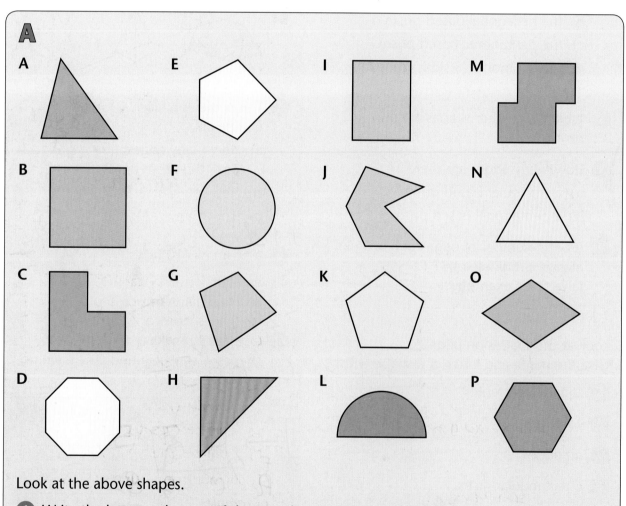

Look at the above shapes.

1 Write the letter and name of the two shapes with curved edges.

2 For each of the shapes with straight edges write:

   a) the letter

   b) the number of sides

   c) the name of the shape.

B

Look at the shapes A to P on page 22.
Give the letter of:

1. a triangle with a right angle

2. a shape with one straight and one curved edge

3. a quadrilateral which is not symmetrical

4. a hexagon with all its edges equal

5. a pentagon with one right angle

6. a triangle with two equal edges

7. a shape with no straight edges

8. a quadrilateral with no right angle but with opposite edges equal

9. a triangle which is not symmetrical

10. a hexagon which is symmetrical but does not have all edges equal

11. a pentagon with all its edges equal

12. a shape with eight edges which is not symmetrical.

13. Start with a rectangle of card. Join the midway points of the shorter sides. Cut along this line.

Put your shapes together to make:
a) 2 different triangles
b) 3 different quadrilaterals
c) 2 different pentagons
d) 2 different hexagons.

Draw round and name your shapes.

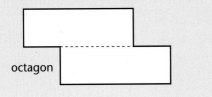

octagon

C

1. Copy the Carroll diagram. Sort the shapes on page 22 by writing the letters in the right places.

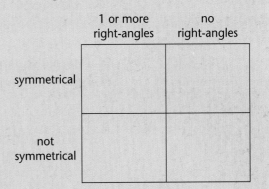

2. Copy the Carroll diagram. Sort the shapes with straight edges only on page 22.

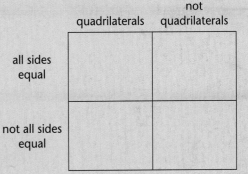

3. Cut a rectangle of card into 2 equal triangles. Put your shapes together to make:

a) 2 different triangles
b) 3 different quadrilaterals
c) 2 different pentagons
d) 2 different hexagons.

Draw round and name your shapes.
Example

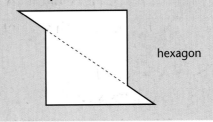

hexagon

I can complete magic squares.

Example

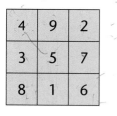

In a magic square the sum of each row, column and diagonal is the same.

(↔) Rows (↔)
4 + 9 + 2 = 15
3 + 5 + 7 = 15
8 + 1 + 6 = 15

(↕) Columns (↕)
4 + 3 + 8 = 15
9 + 5 + 1 = 15
2 + 7 + 6 = 15

(↗) Diagonals (↘)
4 + 5 + 6 = 15
8 + 5 + 2 = 15

A
Copy and complete the following magic squares.

❶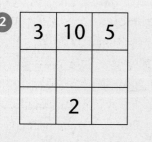

❷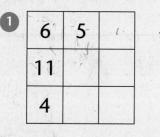

❸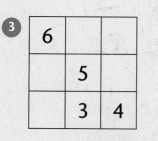

B
Copy and complete the following magic squares.

❶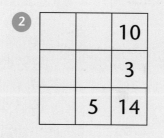

❷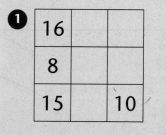

❸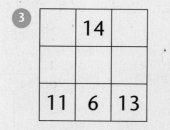

C
Copy and complete the following magic squares.

❶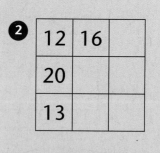

❷ (magic square: 12 16 _; 20 _ _; 13 _ _)

❸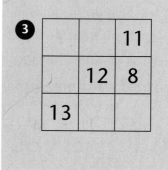

I can show information in a frequency table and use a frequency table to find information.

Example

The ages of children in a basketball club

```
10   9   8  10   9  10  11
 8  10  11   9  10   8  10
 9  10  10   8  11  10   9
10  11   9  10   8   9  10
```

A frequency table showing the ages.

Ages	No. of children
8	5
9	7
10	12
11	4

A

The children in a class voted for their favourite type of potatoes. The frequency table shows the results.

Potatoes	Votes
Boiled	3
Jacket	6
Mashed	4
Roast	7

1. What was the most popular type of potato?

2. What was the least popular?

3. How many children voted for jacket potatoes?

4. Which type of potato was voted for by 4 children?

5. How many more children chose roast potatoes than mashed?

6. How many children voted?

B

Class 3 chose the new colour for their classroom walls. They chose from blue, cream, green, white and yellow. These are the results of their vote.

```
B  Y  W  C  Y  B  C
Y  G  C  Y  W  C  B
C  W  C  B  C  Y  C
B  C  Y  G  Y  W  C
```

1. How many children voted?

2. Make a frequency table to show the results.

3. Check that the numbers of voters in your table adds up to the number of children who voted?

4. Which two colours were:
   a) the most popular
   b) the least popular?

5. How many more children voted for:
   a) cream than blue
   b) yellow than white?

C

For a playtime snack Year 3 can bring one fruit to school from a list of apples, bananas, cherries, grapes and oranges. On one day these were the fruits brought.

```
G  B  C  A  G  B  O  A
A  O  A  B  C  O  G  B
C  A  B  G  A  B  A  O
A  G  O  B  G  O  C  A
G  A  B  C  B  A  O  G
```

1. How many children brought fruit?

2. Make a frequency table to show how many of each fruit were brought to school.

3. Check that the sum of the numbers in your table matches the number of children who brought fruit.

4. How many fewer children brought an orange than an apple?

I can place things on a Venn diagram.

A Venn diagram is used to sort numbers, shapes or objects into groups.

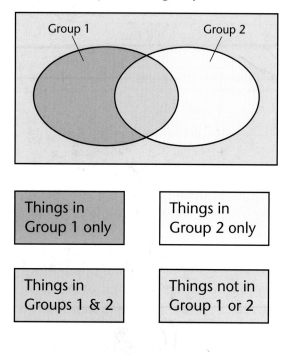

| Group 1 | Group 2 |

| Things in Group 1 only | Things in Group 2 only |
| Things in Groups 1 & 2 | Things not in Group 1 or 2 |

Example

Sort these numbers into a Venn diagram showing multiples of 3 and multiples of 5.

```
 2    5    8   10
12   15   18   20
22   25   28   30
```

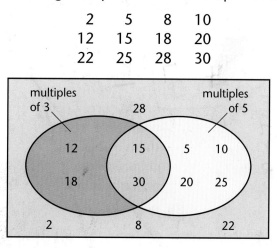

A

1 Copy the Venn diagram and use it to sort these multiples of 5 by writing them in the right place.

```
 5   20   35   50
10   25   40   55
15   30   45   60
```

Even numbers

2 Copy the Venn diagram.
Use it to sort these shapes by writing the letters in the right places.

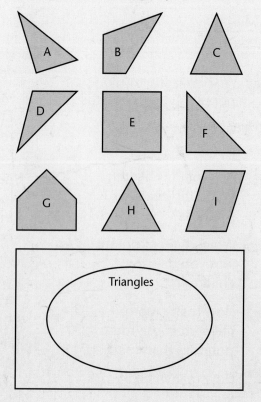

Triangles

B

1 Copy the Venn diagram.
Use it to sort the numbers 1 to 30.

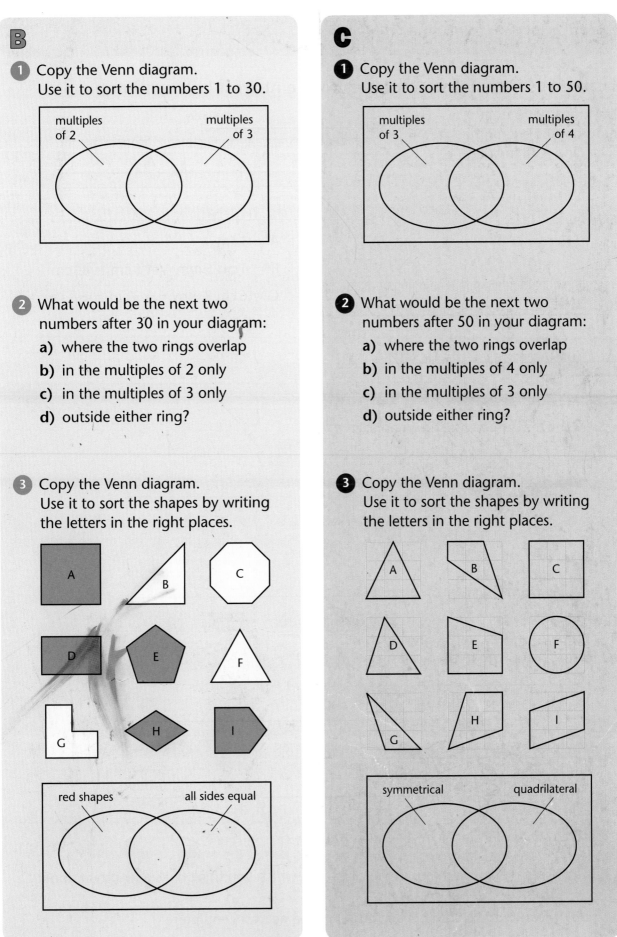

2 What would be the next two
numbers after 30 in your diagram:

a) where the two rings overlap

b) in the multiples of 2 only

c) in the multiples of 3 only

d) outside either ring?

3 Copy the Venn diagram.
Use it to sort the shapes by writing
the letters in the right places.

C

1 Copy the Venn diagram.
Use it to sort the numbers 1 to 50.

2 What would be the next two
numbers after 50 in your diagram:

a) where the two rings overlap

b) in the multiples of 4 only

c) in the multiples of 3 only

d) outside either ring?

3 Copy the Venn diagram.
Use it to sort the shapes by writing
the letters in the right places.

I can measure lengths accurately to the nearest half centimetre.

Start measuring from 0, not from the end of the ruler, and read the scale.

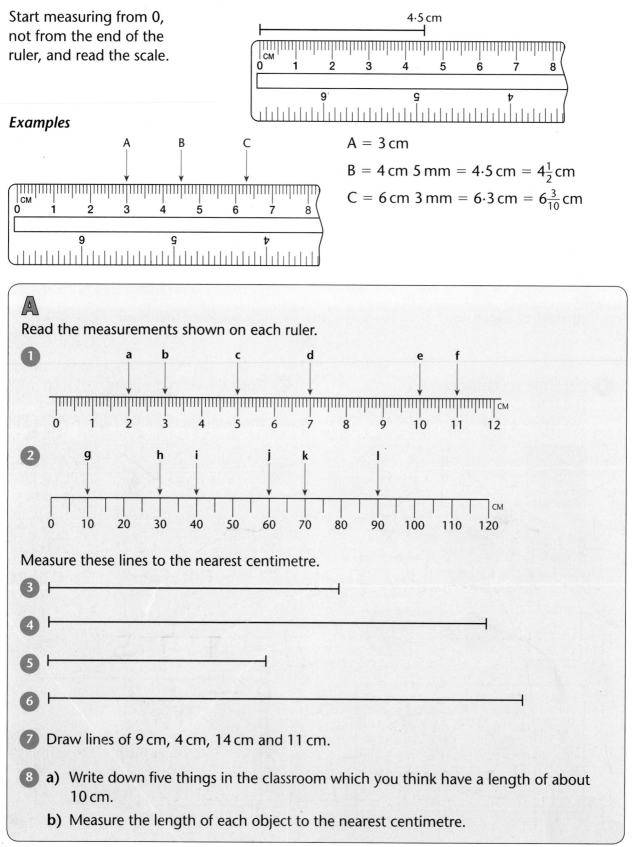

Examples

A = 3 cm

B = 4 cm 5 mm = 4·5 cm = $4\frac{1}{2}$ cm

C = 6 cm 3 mm = 6·3 cm = $6\frac{3}{10}$ cm

A

Read the measurements shown on each ruler.

1

2

Measure these lines to the nearest centimetre.

3

4

5

6

7 Draw lines of 9 cm, 4 cm, 14 cm and 11 cm.

8 a) Write down five things in the classroom which you think have a length of about 10 cm.

   b) Measure the length of each object to the nearest centimetre.

B

Read the measurements shown on each ruler.

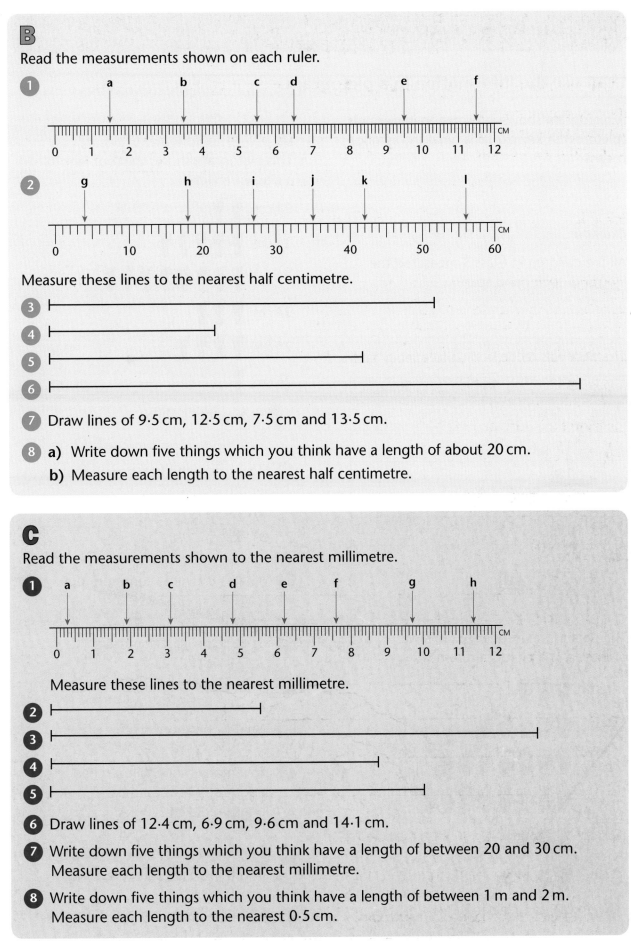

1

2

Measure these lines to the nearest half centimetre.

3

4

5

6

7 Draw lines of 9·5 cm, 12·5 cm, 7·5 cm and 13·5 cm.

8 **a)** Write down five things which you think have a length of about 20 cm.

   b) Measure each length to the nearest half centimetre.

C

Read the measurements shown to the nearest millimetre.

1

Measure these lines to the nearest millimetre.

2

3

4

5

6 Draw lines of 12·4 cm, 6·9 cm, 9·6 cm and 14·1 cm.

7 Write down five things which you think have a length of between 20 and 30 cm.
Measure each length to the nearest millimetre.

8 Write down five things which you think have a length of between 1 m and 2 m.
Measure each length to the nearest 0·5 cm.

I can use the information in a pictogram.

A pictogram shows information in symbols (pictures). A key explains what the symbol means.

Example

All the children in Class 3 measured the length of their hand span.

The data was recorded in a frequency table.

Hand span (cm)	Number of children
$14\frac{1}{2}$	3
15	5
$15\frac{1}{2}$	7
16	8
$16\frac{1}{2}$	4
17	2

The data in the frequency table was displayed in a pictogram.

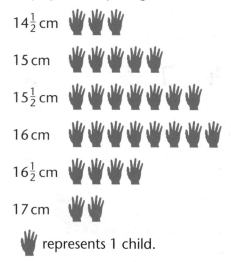

represents 1 child.

A

This pictogram shows the foot length of a class of children.

21 cm 🦶🦶

22 cm 🦶🦶🦶🦶🦶

23 cm 🦶🦶🦶🦶🦶🦶🦶

24 cm 🦶🦶🦶

25 cm 🦶🦶🦶

26 cm 🦶

🦶 represents 1 child.

1 How many children have a foot length of:

   a) 22 cm

   b) 25 cm?

2 What is the most common foot length?

3 What is the least common?

4 What is the longest foot length?

5 What is the shortest?

6 How many more children had a foot length of 23 cm than had a foot length of 24 cm?

7 How many fewer children had a foot length of 26 cm than of 25 cm?

8 How many children are in the class?

B

This pictogram shows the shoe size of children in Class 3.

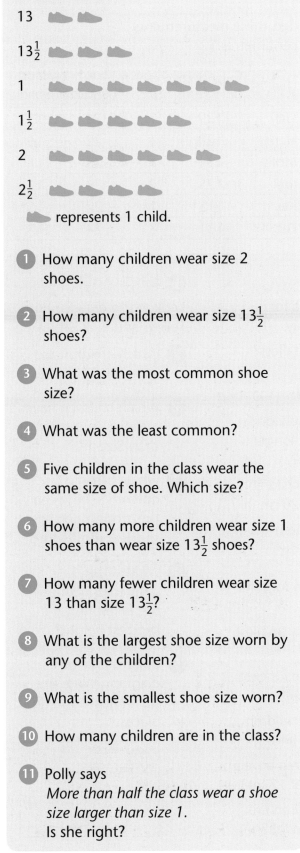

represents 1 child.

1. How many children wear size 2 shoes.

2. How many children wear size $13\frac{1}{2}$ shoes?

3. What was the most common shoe size?

4. What was the least common?

5. Five children in the class wear the same size of shoe. Which size?

6. How many more children wear size 1 shoes than wear size $13\frac{1}{2}$ shoes?

7. How many fewer children wear size 13 than size $13\frac{1}{2}$?

8. What is the largest shoe size worn by any of the children?

9. What is the smallest shoe size worn?

10. How many children are in the class?

11. Polly says
    More than half the class wear a shoe size larger than size 1.
    Is she right?

C

The children in Year 3 voted for their favourite footwear. The results were presented in a pictogram.

Dancing shoes	🧍🧍🧍
Flip flops	🧍🧍🧍🧍🧍
Football boots	🧍🧍🧍
Roller boots	🧍🧍🧍🧍🧍
Wellies	🧍🧍🧍🧍

🧍 represents 2 children.

1. Which footwear was voted for by:
   a) 10 children   b) 6 children?

2. How many children voted for:
   a) football boots   b) flip flops?

3. How many more children voted for:
   a) roller boots than wellies
   b) flip flops than dancing shoes?

4. How many fewer children voted for:
   a) football boots than wellies
   b) flip flops than roller boots?

5. How many children are there in Year 3?

6. The children also voted for their favourite headwear.

Headwear	Number of children
balaclava	6
baseball hat	14
cycle helmet	8
sunhat	12
woolly hat	10

Draw a pictogram to show the results.

I can find information in a table.

The children on Yellow Table and Pink Table recorded these measurements.
(Height, foot length and hand span are shown in centimetres.)

Name	Height	Shoe Size	Foot Length	Hand Span
Ahmed	120	13	22	15
Beth	138	2	24	17
Colin	116	12	21	16
Dee	127	13	22	15
Elton	130	2	23	17
Fiona	118	13	21	16

Name	Height	Shoe Size	Foot Length	Hand Span
Gill	129	1	24	17
Henry	120	1	22	16
India	134	1	23	17
Joel	125	2	23	17
Kay	115	1	22	15
Leo	131	3	24	17

A

Look at the data for Yellow Table. Write down:

1. Ahmed's height
2. Beth's shoe size
3. Dee's foot length
4. Fiona's hand span.

On Yellow Table, who has:

5. a height of 127 cm
6. a shoe size of 12
7. a foot length of 23 cm
8. a hand span of 16 cm?

Look at the data for Pink Table. Write down:

9. Henry's shoe size
10. Leo's hand span
11. Kay's height
12. Gill's foot length

On Pink Table, who has:

13. a hand span of 16 cm
14. a height of 129 cm
15. a foot length of 23 cm
16. a shoe size of 3?

B

Look at the data for Yellow Table only.

1. Who is the tallest?
2. Who has the smallest hand span?
3. How many children have a foot longer than 22 cm?
4. How many children are under 120 cm tall?
5. Which children have Size 13 shoes?

Look at the data for Pink Table only.

6. Who has the smallest hand span?
7. Who has the longest foot?
8. How many children wear Size 1 shoes?
9. Which children have a hand span of 17 cm?
10. Which children are over 130 cm tall?

C

Look at the data for both Yellow and Pink Tables.

1. Which children are less than 125 cm tall?
2. Which children have a shoe size greater than Size 1?
3. What is the difference between the longest and the shortest foot length?
4. What is the difference between the tallest and the shortest height?
5. Copy the Venn diagram. Write the 12 names in the right places.

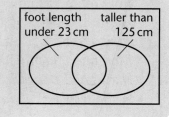

foot length under 23 cm   taller than 125 cm

I can use a range of calculation strategies to solve problems.

Example
Kermit jumps 47 cm.
Fergie jumps 8 cm longer.
How far does Fergie jump?

47 + 8 = 55

Fergie jumps 55 cm.

A

1. A plank of wood is 90 cm long. 60 cm is sawn off. How long is the plank now?

2. Maisie has two 20ps. How much does she have altogether?

3. One dumbbell weighs 30 kg. The other weighs half as much. What is the weight of the two dumbbells added together?

4. Sammy the snake is 63 cm long. Susan is 8 cm longer. How long is Susan?

5. There is 26 litres of water in a bath. Nine litres came from the cold water tap. How much water came from the hot water tap?

B

1. It is 200 m from Leah's house to the school. The post office is 89 m closer. How far is it from Leah's house to the post office?

2. A jug contains 500 ml of lemonade. 300 ml is poured out. How much is left in the jug?

3. Jonathan has eight £5 notes. How much does he have altogether?

4. A full fish tank holds 28 litres of water. The tank is only half full. How much water is in the tank?

5. Keith's father weighs 75 kg. Keith weighs 40 kg less. How much does Keith weigh?

6. Danielle has 65p. Lorette has 9p. How much do they have altogether?

C

1. Winston buys a pencil case for 39p. He pays £1. How much change will he receive?

2. 60 cm of string is cut into 3 equal lengths. How long is each length?

3. A builder loads 43 kg of sand into his van. He adds 26 kg of cement. What is the combined weight of the sand and the cement?

4. There is 150 ml of perfume in one bottle. How much perfume is there in four bottles?

5. Mylee has ten coins. They are all the same. They make £2. What are the coins?

6. A shop has 58 litres of ice cream. 19 litres is sold. How much ice cream is left?

I can recognise and develop a pattern of similar calculations.

A

Continue the pattern from:

1 6 + 10 = 16
16 + 10 = 26
26 + 10 = 36
to
86 + 10 = 96

2 91 − 10 = 81
81 − 10 = 71
71 − 10 = 61
to
11 − 10 = 1

3 An adult ticket for an ice show costs £22. Children pay £10. How much would the tickets cost for:

a) 1 adult and 1 child

b) 1 adult and 2 children

c) 1 adult and 3 children?

4 A piece of string is 75 cm long. Sasha cuts 10 cm lengths from it. How long is the string after Sasha cuts:

a) 1 length of 10 cm

b) 2 lengths of 10 cm

c) 3 lengths of 10 cm?

B

Continue the pattern from:

1 15 + 20 = 35
35 + 20 = ☐
to
95 + 20 = 115

2 126 − 20 = 106
106 − 20 = 86
to
26 − 20 = 6

3 There is 250 ml of medicine in a bottle. Remy takes 20 ml every day. How much medicine is left after:

a) one day

b) two days

c) three days

d) four days?

4 A short brick is 12 cm long. A long brick is 20 cm long. What would be the length of:

a) 1 short and 1 long brick

b) 1 short and 2 long bricks

c) 1 short and 3 long bricks

d) 1 short and 4 long bricks?

C

Continue the pattern from:

1 35 + 200 = 235
235 + 200 = ☐
to
1035 + 200 = 1235

2 1000 − 110 = 890
890 − 110 = 780
780 − 110 = ☐
to
120 − 110 = 10

3 A box weighs 45 g. Each can weighs 120 g. What is the weight of both box and cans if there is:

a) 1 can in the box

b) 2 cans in the box

c) 3 cans in the box

d) 4 cans in the box?

4 A bottle has 750 ml of orange squash. A glass holds 150 ml. How much drink is left in the bottle after:

a) 1 glass is poured

b) 2 glasses are poured

c) 3 glasses are poured

d) 4 glasses are poured

e) 5 glasses are poured?

I can use my knowledge of the metric units to suggest suitable units to measure lengths, weights or capacities.

UNITS OF LENGTH
100 cm = 1 m
1000 m = 1 km

UNITS OF WEIGHT
1000 g = 1 kg

UNITS OF CAPACITY
1000 ml = 1 litre

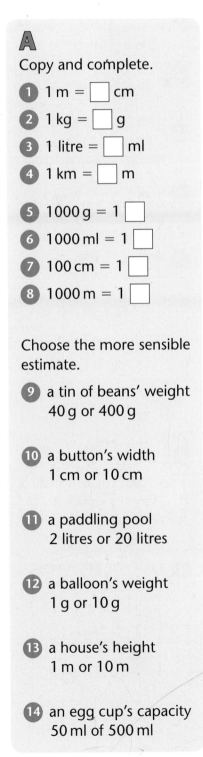

A

Copy and complete.

1 1 m = ☐ cm

2 1 kg = ☐ g

3 1 litre = ☐ ml

4 1 km = ☐ m

5 1000 g = 1 ☐

6 1000 ml = 1 ☐

7 100 cm = 1 ☐

8 1000 m = 1 ☐

Choose the more sensible estimate.

9 a tin of beans' weight
   40 g or 400 g

10 a button's width
   1 cm or 10 cm

11 a paddling pool
   2 litres or 20 litres

12 a balloon's weight
   1 g or 10 g

13 a house's height
   1 m or 10 m

14 an egg cup's capacity
   50 ml of 500 ml

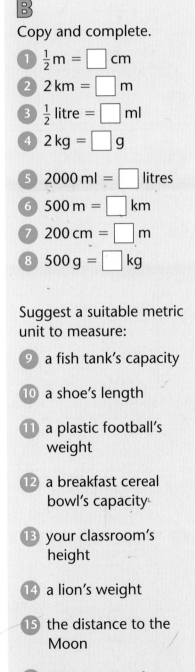

B

Copy and complete.

1 ½ m = ☐ cm

2 2 km = ☐ m

3 ½ litre = ☐ ml

4 2 kg = ☐ g

5 2000 ml = ☐ litres

6 500 m = ☐ km

7 200 cm = ☐ m

8 500 g = ☐ kg

Suggest a suitable metric unit to measure:

9 a fish tank's capacity

10 a shoe's length

11 a plastic football's weight

12 a breakfast cereal bowl's capacity

13 your classroom's height

14 a lion's weight

15 the distance to the Moon

16 the capacity of a kettle.

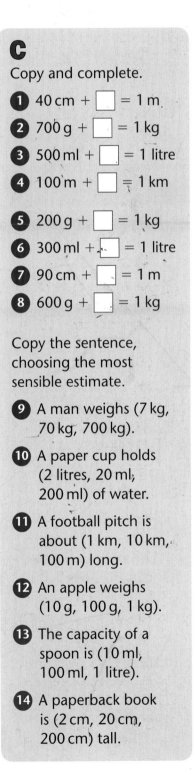

C

Copy and complete.

1 40 cm + ☐ = 1 m

2 700 g + ☐ = 1 kg

3 500 ml + ☐ = 1 litre

4 100 m + ☐ = 1 km

5 200 g + ☐ = 1 kg

6 300 ml + ☐ = 1 litre

7 90 cm + ☐ = 1 m

8 600 g + ☐ = 1 kg

Copy the sentence, choosing the most sensible estimate.

9 A man weighs (7 kg, 70 kg, 700 kg).

10 A paper cup holds (2 litres, 20 ml, 200 ml) of water.

11 A football pitch is about (1 km, 10 km, 100 m) long.

12 An apple weighs (10 g, 100 g, 1 kg).

13 The capacity of a spoon is (10 ml, 100 ml, 1 litre).

14 A paperback book is (2 cm, 20 cm, 200 cm) tall.

I can read scales to the nearest division or half-division.

Work out the measurement shown by each arrow.

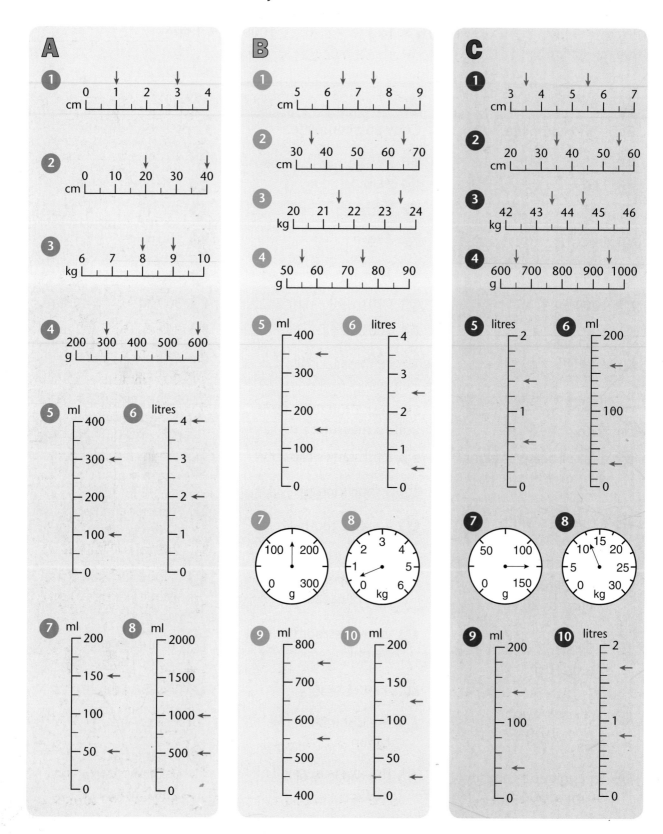

I can use the relationships between seconds, minutes, hours and days.

60 seconds = 1 minute
60 minutes = 1 hour
24 hours = 1 day

Example
How many minutes are left in
the hour if the time is 8:25?
Answer   *35 minutes* (60 − 25)

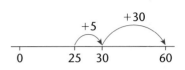

A

How many seconds make:

1 1 minute

2 half a minute

3 one and a half
minutes

4 two minutes?

How many minutes make:

5 one hour

6 half an hour

7 a quarter of an hour

8 three quarters of an
hour?

How many minutes are
left in the hour if the time
is:

9 a quarter past

10 half past

11 a quarter to

12 twenty past?

How many hours make:

13 1 day

14 2 days

15 one half of a day

16 one quarter of a day?

B

How many seconds make:

1 a quarter of a minute

2 two and a half
minutes

3 ten minutes

4 one and a quarter
minutes?

How many minutes make:

5 two hours

6 two and a half hours

7 one and a quarter hours

8 one and a half hours?

How many minutes are left
in the hour if the time is:

9 9:50   **13** 6:20

10 5:25   **14** 1:55

11 11:35   **15** 8:05

12 4:10   **16** 3:40?

How many hours are left in
the day if the time is:

17 10:00 at night

18 3:00 in the afternoon

19 7:00 in the evening

20 8:00 in the morning?

C

How many minutes are:

1 180 seconds

2 300 seconds

3 480 seconds

4 210 seconds?

How many hours are:

5 240 minutes

6 600 minutes

7 20 minutes

8 195 minutes?

How many minutes are
left in the hour if the time
is:

9 10:24   **13** 4:17

10 2:51   **14** 9:32

11 12:08   **15** 5:29

12 7:43   **16** 1:06?

How many hours and
minutes are left in the
day if the time is:

17 3:57 in the afternoon

18 11:34 in the morning

19 8:49 in the evening

20 6:12 in the morning?

I can read the time to the nearest five minutes on a digital clock and on an analogue clock.

Analogue clocks have faces
Read the minutes as:
past before 30 minutes
to after 30 minutes.

Examples

5 minutes past 8   25 minutes to 3

Digital clocks have figures only.
The minutes are always shown as
minutes past the hour

am means before 12 noon
pm means after 12 noon

morning   afternoon
8:05 am   2:35 pm

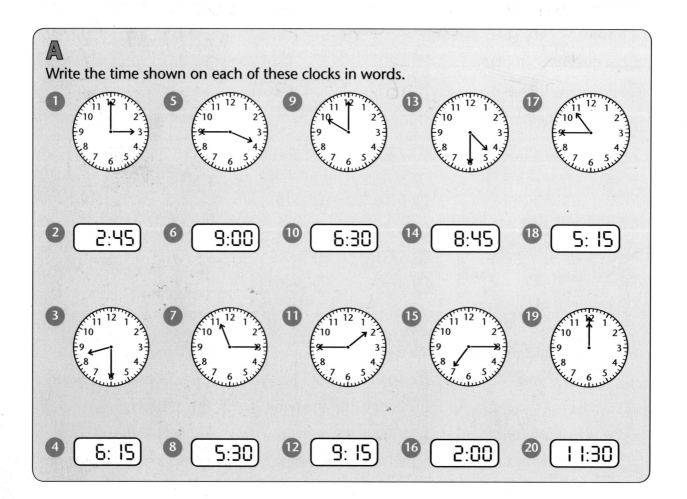

A
Write the time shown on each of these clocks in words.

1.

2. 2:45
3.
4. 6:15

5.
6. 9:00
7.
8. 5:30

9.
10. 6:30
11.
12. 9:15

13.
14. 8:45
15.
16. 2:00

17.
18. 5:15
19.
20. 11:30

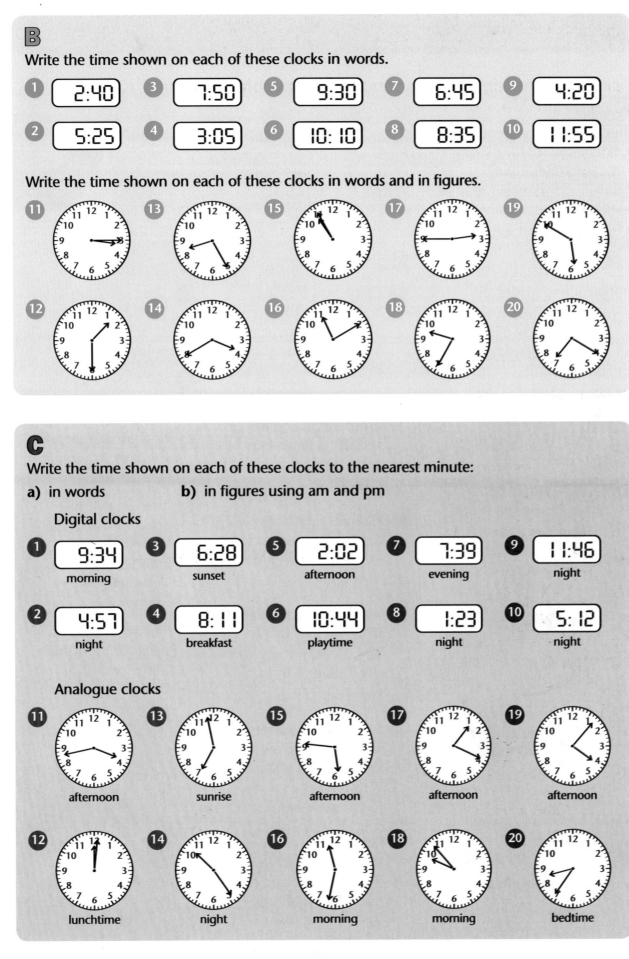

B

Write the time shown on each of these clocks in words.

1. 2:40
2. 5:25
3. 7:50
4. 3:05
5. 9:30
6. 10:10
7. 6:45
8. 8:35
9. 4:20
10. 11:55

Write the time shown on each of these clocks in words and in figures.

11. 12. 13. 14. 15. 16. 17. 18. 19. 20.

C

Write the time shown on each of these clocks to the nearest minute:

a) in words   b) in figures using am and pm

Digital clocks

1. 9:34 morning
2. 4:57 night
3. 6:28 sunset
4. 8:11 breakfast
5. 2:02 afternoon
6. 10:44 playtime
7. 7:39 evening
8. 1:23 night
9. 11:46 night
10. 5:12 night

Analogue clocks

11. afternoon
12. lunchtime
13. sunrise
14. night
15. afternoon
16. morning
17. afternoon
18. morning
19. afternoon
20. bedtime

I can work out time differences to solve problems.

Example
The Music Lesson begins at 9:40.
It finishes at 10:30.
How long does it last?
Answer   *50 minutes* (20 mins. + 30 mins.)

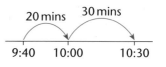

20 mins   30 mins

9:40   10:00   10:30

A

1. Lucy went into the shop at 11:15. She came out at 11:30. How long was she in the shop?

2. A lesson begins at 1:30. It finishes at 2:00. How long does it last?

3. Larry sets off for school at 8:15. He arrives at 8:45. How long does his journey take?

4. Frank begins his drawing at 10:45. He finishes it at 11:00. How long did it take him to draw?

5. The wedding begins at 12:15. It finishes at 1:00. How long does it last?

B

1. Chloe puts a cake in the oven at 10:45. She takes it out at 11:15. How long is it in the oven?

2. A television programme begins at 5:30. It finishes at 6:10. How long does it last?

3. Assembly starts at 9:35. It finishes at 10:10. How long does it last?

4. Terry leaves school at 3:50. He gets home at 4:05. How long does it take him to walk home?

5. A train leaves Oxford at 12:45. It arrives in London at 1:30. How long does the journey take?

6. Maya's watch shows the time as 8:20. The real time is 7:55. How many minutes fast is Maya's watch?

C

1. The Gym Club lasts 70 minutes. It starts at 3:30. When does it finish?

2. Keith sees that the time is 6:10. He realises he has been reading for 40 minutes. When did he start reading?

3. The coach leaves school at 10:18. It arrives at the museum at 11:00. How long did the journey take?

4. The School Sports will take 90 minutes. They should finish at 2:55. When should they start?

5. A film starts at 5:10. It lasts 1 hour and 40 minutes. When does it finish?

6. A football match kicks off at 3:20. The final whistle is blown at 4:35. How long has the match taken?

I can find and describe the position of a square on a labelled grid.

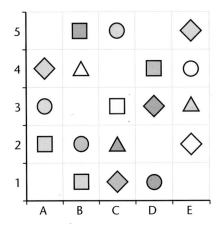

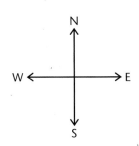

Example
Start at A2.
Go East 2 squares.
Now go North 3 squares.
Draw the symbol.

Answer ◯

A

Use the above grid.
Draw the symbol found
on each of these squares.

1. E4
2. A2
3. C1
4. E3
5. D3
6. C5
7. A4
8. B2

Follow the directions.
Draw the symbol you
find.

9. Start at C2.
Go North 3 squares.

10. Start at E5.
Go West 2 squares.

11. Start at A4.
Go East 4 squares.

12. Start at B5.
Go South 3 squares.

13. Start at D1.
Go North 2 squares.

14. Start at E4.
Go West 3 squares.

B

Use the above grid.
Give the positions of
these symbols.

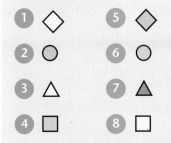

Follow the directions.
Draw the symbol you
find at the end.

9. Start at B5.
South 3 squares.
East 3 squares.

10. Start at A2.
East 4 squares.
North 3 squares.

11. Start at D4.
West 3 squares.
South 2 squares.

12. Start at D1.
North 4 squares.
West 2 squares.

C

Use squared paper.
Label an 8 × 8 grid as
above.
Shade each set of
squares to form letters.

1. F7 F6 F5 G5

2. F3 G3 H3 G2 G1

3. B2 C2 D2 D3 D4
C4 B4 B3

4. A6 A7 A8 B7 C6
C7 C8

5. Label another 8 × 8
grid. Use the squares
to shade your initial
letters. Give the
positions of the
squares for each letter.

I can count on and back in regular steps and complete number sequences.

To find the rule that links the numbers look at the gaps.

Examples

2 4 6 8 10   The rule is *add 2*.

20 16 12 8 4   The rule is *subtract 4*.

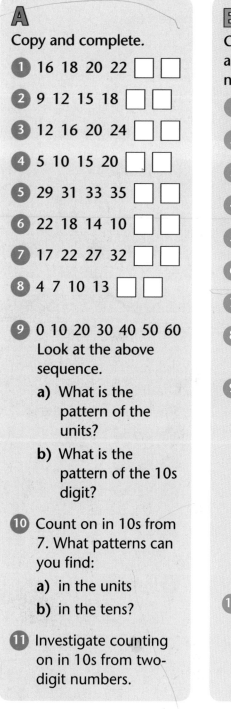

A

Copy and complete.

1 16 18 20 22 ☐ ☐

2 9 12 15 18 ☐ ☐

3 12 16 20 24 ☐ ☐

4 5 10 15 20 ☐ ☐

5 29 31 33 35 ☐ ☐

6 22 18 14 10 ☐ ☐

7 17 22 27 32 ☐ ☐

8 4 7 10 13 ☐ ☐

9 0 10 20 30 40 50 60
Look at the above sequence.

a) What is the pattern of the units?

b) What is the pattern of the 10s digit?

10 Count on in 10s from 7. What patterns can you find:

a) in the units

b) in the tens?

11 Investigate counting on in 10s from two-digit numbers.

B

Copy the sequences and write the next three numbers.

1 17 19 21 23

2 30 34 38 42

3 9 14 19 24

4 937 837 737 637

5 51 49 47 45

6 16 26 36 46

7 63 66 69 72

8 84 74 64 54

9 0 5 10 15 20 25
Look at the above sequence.

a) What is the pattern of the units?

b) What is the pattern of the 10s?

10 Count on in 5s from other one-digit and two-digit numbers. What patterns can you find?

C

Write the first six numbers in each sequence.

	Start at	Rule
1	19	+3
2	180	−20
3	12	+6
4	72	−9
5	40	+8
6	86	−11
7	20	+30
8	70	−7

9 Count on in 2s from any even number, including two-digit and three-digit numbers. What patterns can you find?

10 Count on in 2s from any odd number. What patterns can you find?

11 Investigate counting on in single-digit steps from different numbers. What patterns can you find?

I can quickly recall the multiplication facts for 2, 5 and 10 and can count on and back from zero in steps of 3, 4 and 6.

A

What is

1. 6×2
2. 3×2
3. 5×2
4. 8×2

5. 7×5
6. 4×5
7. 10×5
8. 9×5

9. 2×10
10. 6×10
11. 10×10
12. 9×10

13. $20 \div 2$
14. $14 \div 2$
15. $8 \div 2$
16. $18 \div 2$

17. $40 \div 5$
18. $25 \div 5$
19. $5 \div 5$
20. $30 \div 5$

21. $70 \div 10$
22. $40 \div 10$
23. $80 \div 10$
24. $30 \div 10$

B

Copy and complete.

1. $\square \times 2 = 16$
2. $\square \times 5 = 15$
3. $\square \times 10 = 60$
4. $\square \times 2 = 10$

5. $\square \times 5 = 40$
6. $\square \times 10 = 70$
7. $\square \div 2 = 9$
8. $\square \div 5 = 2$

9. $\square \div 10 = 10$
10. $\square \div 2 = 7$
11. $\square \div 5 = 9$
12. $\square \div 10 = 2$

Write the answer only.

13. 4×3
14. 7×3
15. 3×3
16. 5×3

17. 10×4
18. 6×4
19. 9×4
20. 7×4

21. 5×6
22. 8×6
23. 2×6
24. 6×6

25. $30 \div 3$
26. $27 \div 3$
27. $18 \div 3$
28. $24 \div 3$

29. $20 \div 4$
30. $8 \div 4$
31. $16 \div 4$
32. $32 \div 4$

33. $18 \div 6$
34. $54 \div 6$
35. $24 \div 6$
36. $42 \div 6$

C

Copy and complete.

1. $\square \times 3 = 18$
2. $\square \times 4 = 20$
3. $\square \times 6 = 42$
4. $\square \times 3 = 27$

5. $\square \times 4 = 32$
6. $\square \times 6 = 60$
7. $\square \div 3 = 5$
8. $\square \div 4 = 7$

9. $\square \div 6 = 6$
10. $\square \div 3 = 8$
11. $\square \div 4 = 9$
12. $\square \div 6 = 8$

Write the answer only.

13. 3×7
14. 9×7
15. 5×7
16. 6×7

17. 4×8
18. 7×8
19. 10×8
20. 8×8

21. 6×9
22. 3×9
23. 8×9
24. 5×9

25. $56 \div 7$
26. $28 \div 7$
27. $14 \div 7$
28. $49 \div 7$

29. $40 \div 8$
30. $24 \div 8$
31. $72 \div 8$
32. $48 \div 8$

33. $63 \div 9$
34. $18 \div 9$
35. $81 \div 9$
36. $36 \div 9$

I can use my knowledge of multiplication facts to answer questions.

Examples

If I have 40p in 10p coins, how many coins do I have?

40 ÷ 10 = 4

Answer   *4 coins*

What is 6 multiplied by 4?

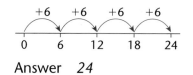

Answer   *24*

A

1. What is 2 multiplied by 6?

2. What is 8 times 5?

3. What is 7 times as big as 10?

4. How many 5s are there in 45?

5. What is 16 shared by 2?

6. What is 60 divided by 10?

7. I have nine 2p coins. How much money do I have?

8. What is the value of five 10p coins?

9. How much is four 5p coins?

10. How many 2p coins make 10p?

11. I have 35p. I have 5p coins only. How many coins do I have?

12. How many 10ps make 90p?

B

1. What is 9 lots of 4?

2. How many 3s make 18?

3. What is 5 multiplied by 6?

4. What is 28 divided by 4?

5. What is seven 3s?

6. How many is 48 shared by 6?

7. One camel has 2 humps. How many humps do seven camels have?

8. How many 10 g weights make 100 g?

9. How many fingers are there on 6 hands?

10. How many teams of 3 can be made from 24 children?

11. There are 6 eggs in each box. I have 36 eggs. How many boxes do I need?

C

1. How many 9s make 45?

2. How much is three 20p coins worth?

3. What is 6 times greater than 7?

4. I use 50 g weights to make 200 g. How many weights do I use?

5. How many days are there in five weeks?

6. What is one eighth of 24?

7. One sweet costs 9p. What do six sweets cost?

8. I put ten 100 g weights on a scale. How much weight is this altogether?

9. There are 32 children in a class. They are divided equally between eight tables. How many children are at each table?

10. Bella's newts have 48 legs altogether. How many newts does she have?

I can identify the shapes made by the multiples of some numbers on a digit wheel.

Examples
Multiples are the numbers in a multiplication table.
The multiples of 2 are 2, 4, 6, 8, 10, 12, etc.
The multiples of 3 are 3, 6, 9, 12, 15, 18, etc.

Do not write in this book

A

Write down the first five multiples of:

1 2   **3** 4

2 5   **4** 10.

5 Which digit do all multiples of 10 end in?

6 Write down the two digits which all multiples of 5 end in.

7 Write down the five digits which all multiples of 2 end in.

Write Yes or No.

8 Is 27 a multiple of 2?

9 Is 75 a multiple of 5?

10 Is 48 a multiple of 10?

11 Is 38 a multiple of 2?

12 Is 56 a multiple of 5?

13 Is 30 a multiple of 10?

14 Is 94 a multiple of 2?

15 Is 40 a multiple of 5?

16 Is 102 a multiple of 10?

B

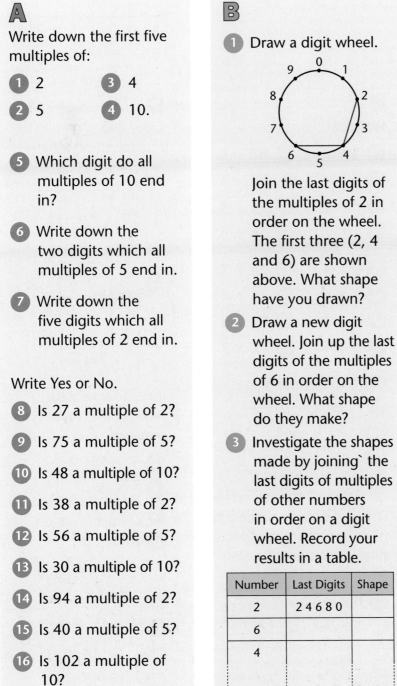

1 Draw a digit wheel.

Join the last digits of the multiples of 2 in order on the wheel. The first three (2, 4 and 6) are shown above. What shape have you drawn?

2 Draw a new digit wheel. Join up the last digits of the multiples of 6 in order on the wheel. What shape do they make?

3 Investigate the shapes made by joining` the last digits of multiples of other numbers in order on a digit wheel. Record your results in a table.

Number	Last Digits	Shape
2	2 4 6 8 0	
6		
4		

C

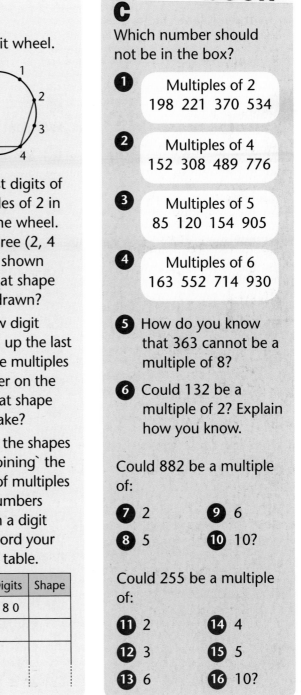

Which number should not be in the box?

1
| Multiples of 2 |
| 198 221 370 534 |

2
| Multiples of 4 |
| 152 308 489 776 |

3
| Multiples of 5 |
| 85 120 154 905 |

4
| Multiples of 6 |
| 163 552 714 930 |

5 How do you know that 363 cannot be a multiple of 8?

6 Could 132 be a multiple of 2? Explain how you know.

Could 882 be a multiple of:

7 2   **9** 6

8 5   **10** 10?

Could 255 be a multiple of:

11 2   **14** 4

12 3   **15** 5

13 6   **16** 10?

I can state three related facts given any multiplication or division fact.

Examples

Multiplication is repeated addition.

$5 \times 3 = 15$

Division is repeated subtraction.

$20 \div 4 = 5$

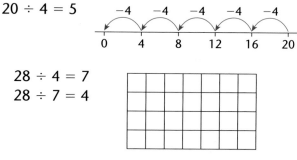

Knowing one multiplication or division fact means that you know three related facts.

$7 \times 4 = 28$	$28 \div 4 = 7$
$4 \times 7 = 28$	$28 \div 7 = 4$

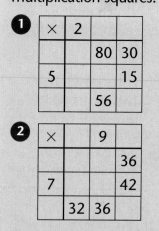

A

Work out

1. 5×2
2. 3×5
3. 6×10
4. 7×2
5. 8×5
6. 10×10
7. 4×2
8. 5×5
9. $30 \div 10$
10. $12 \div 2$
11. $20 \div 5$
12. $80 \div 10$
13. $18 \div 2$
14. $35 \div 5$
15. $40 \div 10$
16. $20 \div 2$

Copy and complete.

17. $\square \times 5 = 45$
18. $\square \times 10 = 50$
19. $\square \div 2 = 8$
20. $\square \div 5 = 6$

Write four facts for each array.

21.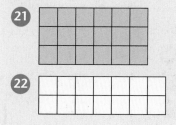

22.

B

Work out

1. 5×3
2. 3×4
3. 6×6
4. 10×3
5. 9×4
6. 5×6
7. 7×3
8. 6×4
9. $48 \div 6$
10. $18 \div 3$
11. $16 \div 4$
12. $54 \div 6$
13. $24 \div 3$
14. $28 \div 4$
15. $24 \div 6$
16. $12 \div 3$

Copy and complete.

17. $\square \times 4 = 20$
18. $\square \times 6 = 42$
19. $\square \div 3 = 9$
20. $\square \div 4 = 8$

Draw an array for each of these facts. Write four related facts next to each array.

21. 8×2
22. 3×7
23. $10 \div 2$
24. $32 \div 4$

C

Copy and complete the multiplication squares.

1.

×	2		
		80	30
5			15
		56	

2.

×		9	
			36
7			42
	32	36	

Write four related facts for each group of numbers.

3. 5 7 35
4. 4 8 32
5. 7 63 9
6. 21 63 3

Copy and complete.

7. $\square \times 7 = 49$
8. $\square \times 5 = 100$
9. $\square \div 8 = 9$
10. $\square \div 50 = 4$

I can divide a number of objects by grouping and work out a remainder.

Example
13 counters are sorted into groups of 4.

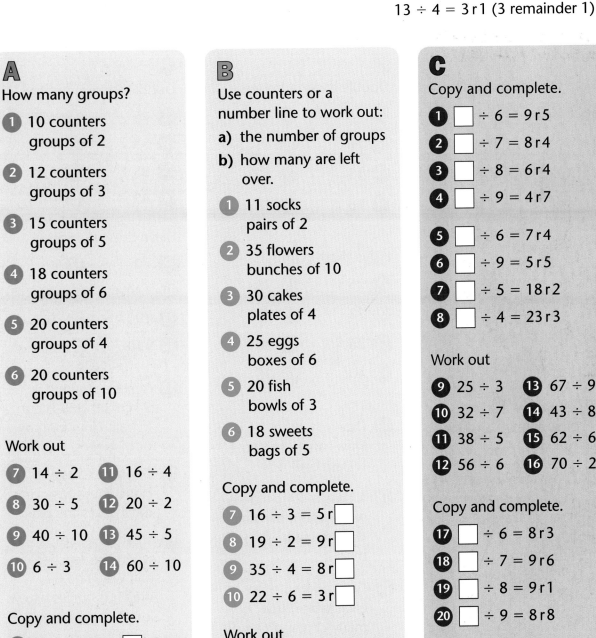

$13 \div 4 = 3\,r\,1$ (3 remainder 1)

A

How many groups?

1 10 counters
   groups of 2

2 12 counters
   groups of 3

3 15 counters
   groups of 5

4 18 counters
   groups of 6

5 20 counters
   groups of 4

6 20 counters
   groups of 10

Work out

7 $14 \div 2$ 11 $16 \div 4$

8 $30 \div 5$ 12 $20 \div 2$

9 $40 \div 10$ 13 $45 \div 5$

10 $6 \div 3$ 14 $60 \div 10$

Copy and complete.

15 $9 = 4 \times 2 + \square$

16 $43 = 8 \times 5 + \square$

17 $76 = 7 \times 10 + \square$

18 $14 = 3 \times 4 + \square$

B

Use counters or a
number line to work out:

a) the number of groups

b) how many are left
    over.

1 11 socks
   pairs of 2

2 35 flowers
   bunches of 10

3 30 cakes
   plates of 4

4 25 eggs
   boxes of 6

5 20 fish
   bowls of 3

6 18 sweets
   bags of 5

Copy and complete.

7 $16 \div 3 = 5\,r\,\square$

8 $19 \div 2 = 9\,r\,\square$

9 $35 \div 4 = 8\,r\,\square$

10 $22 \div 6 = 3\,r\,\square$

Work out

11 $17 \div 2$ 15 $22 \div 3$

12 $15 \div 4$ 16 $16 \div 6$

13 $27 \div 5$ 17 $25 \div 4$

14 $68 \div 10$ 18 $42 \div 5$

C

Copy and complete.

1 $\square \div 6 = 9\,r\,5$

2 $\square \div 7 = 8\,r\,4$

3 $\square \div 8 = 6\,r\,4$

4 $\square \div 9 = 4\,r\,7$

5 $\square \div 6 = 7\,r\,4$

6 $\square \div 9 = 5\,r\,5$

7 $\square \div 5 = 18\,r\,2$

8 $\square \div 4 = 23\,r\,3$

Work out

9 $25 \div 3$ 13 $67 \div 9$

10 $32 \div 7$ 14 $43 \div 8$

11 $38 \div 5$ 15 $62 \div 6$

12 $56 \div 6$ 16 $70 \div 20$

Copy and complete.

17 $\square \div 6 = 8\,r\,3$

18 $\square \div 7 = 9\,r\,6$

19 $\square \div 8 = 9\,r\,1$

20 $\square \div 9 = 8\,r\,8$

21 $\square \div 6 = 3\,r\,1$

22 $\square \div 7 = 5\,r\,3$

23 $\square \div 8 = 7\,r\,5$

24 $\square \div 9 = 10\,r\,3$

I can quickly find doubles of all numbers to 20.

Examples

Double 14
10 × 2 add 4 × 2
20 add 8
28

Half of 36
30 ÷ 2 add 6 ÷ 2   or
15 add 3
18

Half of 36
20 ÷ 2 add 16 ÷ 2
10 add 8
18

A

Write the answers only.

1 5 × 2   5 6 × 2

2 7 × 2   6 4 × 2

3 2 × 2   7 9 × 2

4 8 × 2   8 3 × 2

Write the answers only.

9 12 ÷ 2   13 8 ÷ 2

10 6 ÷ 2   14 14 ÷ 2

11 10 ÷ 2   15 20 ÷ 2

12 18 ÷ 2   16 4 ÷ 2

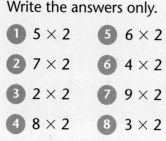

17 Jay has 14 socks. How many pairs does he have?

18 There are 9 sweets in a small packet. A large packet has twice as many. How many sweets are there in a large packet?

19 There are 16 children at a party. One half are boys. How many girls are at the party?

20 How many skis are needed for 6 people?

B

Double these numbers.

1 12   5 20

2 16   6 11

3 13   7 17

4 18   8 14

Halve these numbers.

9 26   13 28

10 22   14 34

11 36   15 30

12 40   16 38

17 One lolly costs 19p. How much do two lollies cost?

18 A class of 24 children work with a partner. How many pairs are there?

19 Two children sit at each table. How many children can sit at 15 tables?

20 There are 32 children in a class. One half are girls. How many boys are there?

C

Double these numbers.

1 25   5 62

2 55   6 74

3 85   7 37

4 45   8 98

Halve these numbers.

9 70   13 46

10 130   14 78

11 190   15 162

12 150   16 114

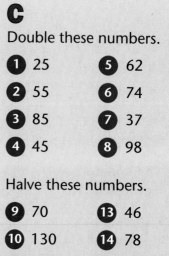

17 A piece of wood is 94 cm long. It is cut in half. How long are both pieces?

18 One pen costs 49p. Honey buys two. How much does she pay?

19 A car driver stops when she reaches half way. She has driven 88 miles. How long is her journey?

20 There are 56 children in Year 3. They are split into two equal classes. How many children are in each class?

I can multiply a two-digit number by a single digit number.

Examples

$16 \times 4 = 10 \times 4$ plus 6×4
$= 40$ plus 24
$= 64$

$23 \times 2 = 20 \times 2$ plus 3×2
$= 40$ plus 6
$= 46$

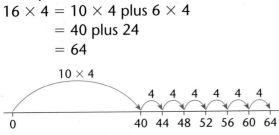

A

Work out

1. 19×2
2. 15×3
3. 13×5
4. 12×4

5. 26×2
6. 11×5
7. 18×3
8. 15×4

9. There are 17 flowers in each bunch. How many flowers are there in three bunches?

10. Gary has eleven conkers. Noel has five times as many. How many conkers does Noel have?

11. Tomatoes are sold in packs of four. There are 22 packs. How many tomatoes are there?

B

Work out

1. 33×3 9. 47×2
2. 21×4 10. 16×3
3. 14×6 11. 25×4
4. 38×2 12. 12×6

5. 16×4 13. 14×5
6. 11×6 14. 31×3
7. 27×3 15. 19×4
8. 19×5 16. 15×6

17. Sixteen teams take part in a 5-a-side football competition. How many players are there?

18. There are three classes of 28 children in Year 2. How many children are there in Year 2?

19. One sweet costs 15p. How much do six sweets cost?

20. One train ticket costs £27. What do four tickets cost?

C

Work out

1. 45×3 9. 79×2
2. 24×6 10. 14×7
3. 58×2 11. 27×5
4. 13×8 12. 46×6

5. 37×5 13. 28×4
6. 22×9 14. 25×8
7. 47×4 15. 32×6
8. 18×6 16. 59×3

17. One biscuit weighs 25 g. What do 6 biscuits weigh?

18. There are 12 eggs in a large box. How many eggs are there in eight large boxes?

19. One stamp costs 39p. What do four stamps cost?

20. How many days are there in 23 weeks?

21. One box holds 48 packets of chewing gum. How many packets are there in five boxes?

I can recognise fractions of shapes.

When a whole one is divided into equal parts each of the parts is a fraction of the whole one.

Examples

2 equal parts

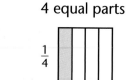

$\frac{1}{2}$

one half is shaded

4 equal parts

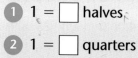

$\frac{1}{4}$

one quarter is shaded

10 equal parts

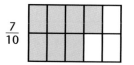

$\frac{7}{10}$

seven tenths is shaded

A

Use a plain piece of paper. Draw 3 rectangles by drawing round a template. The rectangles must be exactly the same. Cut out the rectangles.

Rectangle 1

Carefully fold in half. Write $\frac{1}{2}$ in each part.

Rectangle 2

Carefully fold into quarters. Write $\frac{1}{4}$ in all four parts.

Rectangle 3

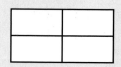

Carefully fold into eighths. Write $\frac{1}{8}$ in all eight parts.

B

Use your shapes from Section A to copy and complete.

1 1 = ☐ halves

2 1 = ☐ quarters

3 1 = ☐ eighths

4 $\frac{1}{2}$ = ☐ quarters

5 $\frac{1}{2}$ = ☐ eighths

6 $\frac{1}{4}$ = ☐ eighths

What fraction of each diagram is shaded?

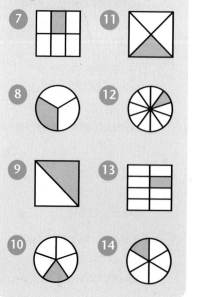

C

What fraction of each diagram is shaded?

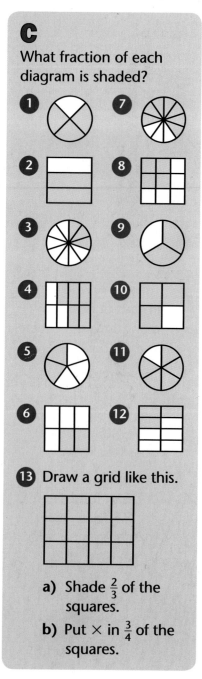

13 Draw a grid like this.

a) Shade $\frac{2}{3}$ of the squares.

b) Put × in $\frac{3}{4}$ of the squares.

I can find $\frac{1}{2}$, $\frac{1}{4}$ or $\frac{1}{8}$ of amounts by repeated halving.

Examples

$\frac{1}{2}$ of 24 = 12 $\frac{1}{4}$ of 24 = 6 $\frac{1}{8}$ of 24 = 3 $\frac{1}{2}$ of £1·60 = 80p

$\frac{1}{4}$ of £1·60 = 40p ($\frac{1}{2}$ of 80p)

$\frac{1}{8}$ of £1·60 = 20p ($\frac{1}{2}$ of 40p)

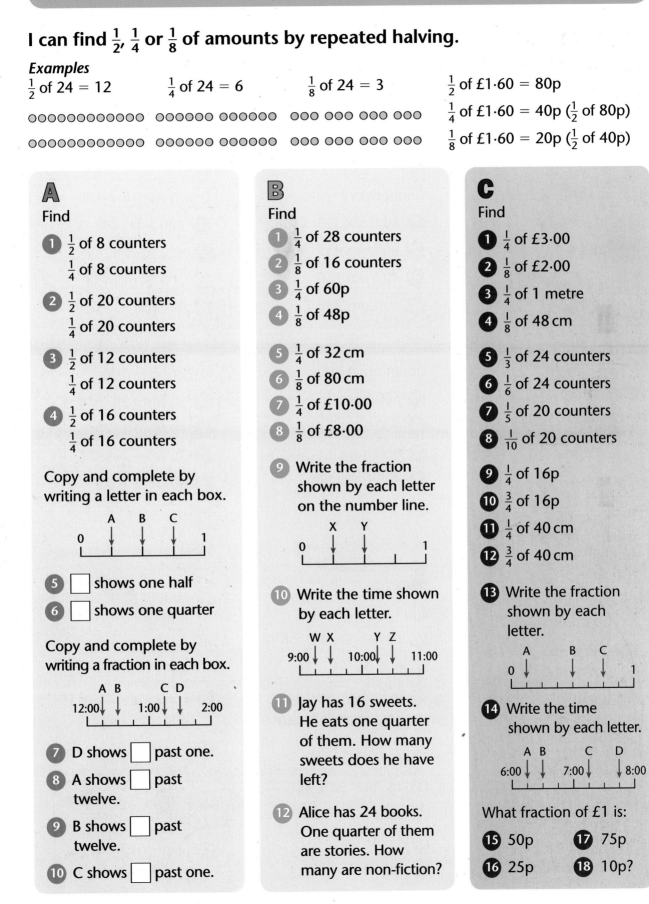

A

Find

1 $\frac{1}{2}$ of 8 counters
   $\frac{1}{4}$ of 8 counters

2 $\frac{1}{2}$ of 20 counters
   $\frac{1}{4}$ of 20 counters

3 $\frac{1}{2}$ of 12 counters
   $\frac{1}{4}$ of 12 counters

4 $\frac{1}{2}$ of 16 counters
   $\frac{1}{4}$ of 16 counters

Copy and complete by writing a letter in each box.

     A   B   C
0   ↓   ↓   ↓   1

5 ☐ shows one half

6 ☐ shows one quarter

Copy and complete by writing a fraction in each box.

       A B   C D
12:00↓ ↓ 1:00↓ ↓ 2:00

7 D shows ☐ past one.

8 A shows ☐ past twelve.

9 B shows ☐ past twelve.

10 C shows ☐ past one.

B

Find

1 $\frac{1}{4}$ of 28 counters

2 $\frac{1}{8}$ of 16 counters

3 $\frac{1}{4}$ of 60p

4 $\frac{1}{8}$ of 48p

5 $\frac{1}{4}$ of 32 cm

6 $\frac{1}{8}$ of 80 cm

7 $\frac{1}{4}$ of £10·00

8 $\frac{1}{8}$ of £8·00

9 Write the fraction shown by each letter on the number line.

        X   Y
0   ↓   ↓   1

10 Write the time shown by each letter.

    W X   Y Z
9:00↓ ↓ 10:00↓ ↓ 11:00

11 Jay has 16 sweets. He eats one quarter of them. How many sweets does he have left?

12 Alice has 24 books. One quarter of them are stories. How many are non-fiction?

C

Find

1 $\frac{1}{4}$ of £3·00

2 $\frac{1}{8}$ of £2·00

3 $\frac{1}{4}$ of 1 metre

4 $\frac{1}{8}$ of 48 cm

5 $\frac{1}{3}$ of 24 counters

6 $\frac{1}{6}$ of 24 counters

7 $\frac{1}{5}$ of 20 counters

8 $\frac{1}{10}$ of 20 counters

9 $\frac{1}{4}$ of 16p

10 $\frac{3}{4}$ of 16p

11 $\frac{1}{4}$ of 40 cm

12 $\frac{3}{4}$ of 40 cm

13 Write the fraction shown by each letter.

     A   B   C
0   ↓   ↓   ↓   1

14 Write the time shown by each letter.

      A B   C   D
6:00 ↓ ↓ 7:00↓   ↓ 8:00

What fraction of £1 is:

15 50p   17 75p

16 25p   18 10p?

Examples

Count on 60 in 10s from 871.

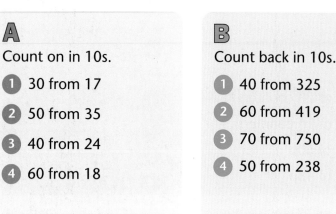

Count back 600 in 100s from 945.

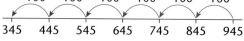

A

Count on in 10s.

1. 30 from 17
2. 50 from 35
3. 40 from 24
4. 60 from 18

Count back in 10s.

5. 20 from 42
6. 50 from 76
7. 30 from 91
8. 40 from 83

Write the first six numbers in each sequence.

9. Start at 9.
   Count on in 2s.
10. Start at 47.
    Count back in 5s.
11. Start at 13.
    Count on in 4s.
12. Start at 32.
    Count back in 3s.
13. Start at 8.
    Count on in 5s.
14. Start at 26.
    Count back in 2s.

B

Count back in 10s.

1. 40 from 325
2. 60 from 419
3. 70 from 750
4. 50 from 238

Count on in 100s.

5. 500 from 262
6. 400 from 594
7. 600 from 131
8. 700 from 276

Write the next three numbers in each sequence.

9. 14 17 20 23
10. 69 67 65 63
11. 0 6 12 18
12. 420 400 380 360
13. 390 340 290 240
14. 62 58 54 50
15. 18 118 218 318
16. 30 60 90 120
17. 41 46 51 56
18. 55 59 63 67

C

Count back in 100s.

1. 300 from 767
2. 600 from 1241
3. 500 from 1438
4. 800 from 1392

Count on in 10s.

5. 50 from 287
6. 40 from 1870
7. 70 from 2436
8. 60 from 1073

What number did I start from?

9. I count back six 25s and reach 104.
10. I count back four 9s and reach 47.
11. I count back five 15s and reach 28.
12. I count back six 7s and reach 51.
13. I count back four 8s and reach 119.
14. I count back five 40s and reach 120.

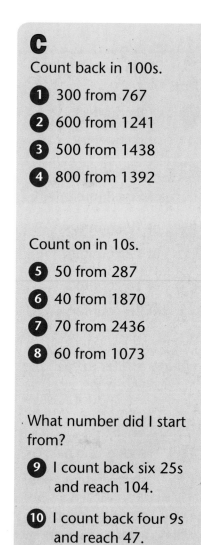

I can round any two-digit number to the nearest 10 and any three-digit number to the nearest 100.

ROUNDING TO THE NEAREST 10
Look at the units column.
5 or more, round up.
Less than 5, round down.

Examples
39 rounds to 40
34 rounds to 30
45 rounds to 50

ROUNDING TO THE NEAREST 100
Look at the tens and units columns.
50 or more, round up.
Less than 50, round down.

Examples
462 rounds to 500
448 rounds to 400
750 rounds to 800

A
Copy and complete.

1. 23 rounds to ☐
2. 78 rounds to ☐
3. 92 rounds to ☐
4. 16 rounds to ☐

5. 44 rounds to ☐
6. 35 rounds to ☐
7. 87 rounds to ☐
8. 69 rounds to ☐

9. 31 rounds to ☐
10. 58 rounds to ☐
11. 43 rounds to ☐
12. 46 rounds to ☐

13. 24 rounds to ☐
14. 75 rounds to ☐
15. 81 rounds to ☐
16. 53 rounds to ☐

B
Round to the nearest 10.

1. 84
2. 37
3. 29
4. 72
5. 13
6. 25
7. 61
8. 48
9. 17
10. 33
11. 65
12. 98
13. 55
14. 74
15. 83
16. 45

Round to the nearest 100.

17. 130
18. 460
19. 380
20. 710
21. 620
22. 850
23. 573
24. 208
25. 952
26. 495
27. 847
28. 796
29. 126
30. 584
31. 339
32. 163

C
Round to the nearest 10.

1. 168
2. 314
3. 289
4. 425
5. 103
6. 97
7. 382
8. 635

Round to the nearest 100.

9. 756
10. 618
11. 1250
12. 2815
13. 3582
14. 1539
15. 2951
16. 1497

Approximate by rounding to the nearest 10.

17. $51 + 28$
18. $39 + 47$
19. $85 - 66$
20. $91 - 38$

Approximate by rounding the first number.

21. 45×2
22. 27×3
23. 62×5
24. 71×4

I can use the vocabulary of estimation and approximation, such as *about*, *between*, *a bit more than* and *a bit less than*.

Examples

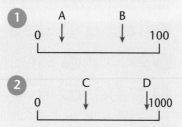

Arrow X is about 40.
Arrow Y is between 80 and 90.

Estimate and then
work out 48 × 3.

48 × 3 is a bit less
than 50 × 3 or 150.

48 × 3 = 50 × 3 take 2 × 3
= 150 take 6
= 144

A

Estimate the number of dots in each box to the nearest 10 by writing a sentence using *about*.

1

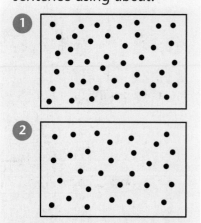

2

Estimate the number of dots in each box to the nearest 10 by writing a sentence using *between*.

3

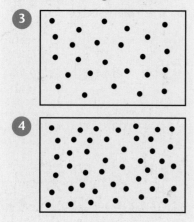

4

B

Estimate the position of each letter by writing a sentence using *about*.

1

A   B
0 ↓   ↓ 100

2

C   D
0 ↓   ↓1000

Estimate the position of each letter by writing a sentence using *between*.

3

E   F
0 ↓   ↓   100

4

G   H
0   ↓   ↓   1000

Use rounding to estimate and then work out.

5 38 + 29   **9** 38 × 2

6 52 + 33   **10** 22 × 5

7 49 − 22   **11** 33 × 4

8 66 − 18   **12** 19 × 3

C

Estimate the position of each letter by writing a sentence using *about*.

1

M   N
400 ↓   ↓500

2

O   P
3000↓   ↓   4000

Estimate the position of each letter by writing a sentence using *between*.

3

Q   R
900 ↓   ↓   1000

4

S   T
500 ↓   ↓1500

Use rounding to estimate and then work out.

5 71 + 64   **9** 58 × 6

6 59 + 47   **10** 79 × 5

7 145 − 67   **11** 64 ÷ 2

8 123 − 49   **12** 87 ÷ 3

I can add or subtract multiples and near multiples of 10 or 100.

Examples

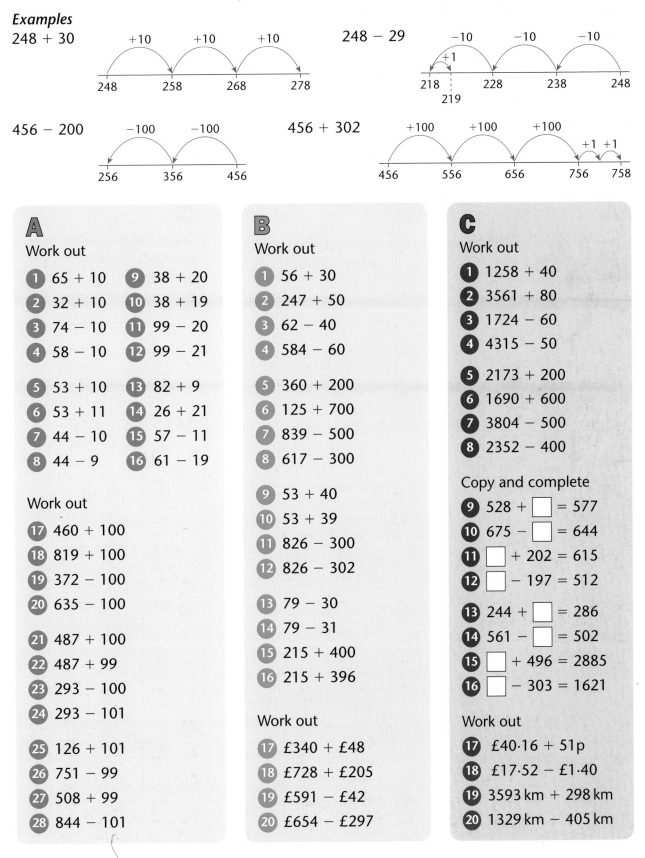

A

Work out

1. 65 + 10
2. 32 + 10
3. 74 − 10
4. 58 − 10

5. 53 + 10
6. 53 + 11
7. 44 − 10
8. 44 − 9

9. 38 + 20
10. 38 + 19
11. 99 − 20
12. 99 − 21

13. 82 + 9
14. 26 + 21
15. 57 − 11
16. 61 − 19

Work out

17. 460 + 100
18. 819 + 100
19. 372 − 100
20. 635 − 100

21. 487 + 100
22. 487 + 99
23. 293 − 100
24. 293 − 101

25. 126 + 101
26. 751 − 99
27. 508 + 99
28. 844 − 101

B

Work out

1. 56 + 30
2. 247 + 50
3. 62 − 40
4. 584 − 60

5. 360 + 200
6. 125 + 700
7. 839 − 500
8. 617 − 300

9. 53 + 40
10. 53 + 39
11. 826 − 300
12. 826 − 302

13. 79 − 30
14. 79 − 31
15. 215 + 400
16. 215 + 396

Work out

17. £340 + £48
18. £728 + £205
19. £591 − £42
20. £654 − £297

C

Work out

1. 1258 + 40
2. 3561 + 80
3. 1724 − 60
4. 4315 − 50

5. 2173 + 200
6. 1690 + 600
7. 3804 − 500
8. 2352 − 400

Copy and complete

9. 528 + ☐ = 577
10. 675 − ☐ = 644
11. ☐ + 202 = 615
12. ☐ − 197 = 512

13. 244 + ☐ = 286
14. 561 − ☐ = 502
15. ☐ + 496 = 2885
16. ☐ − 303 = 1621

Work out

17. £40·16 + 51p
18. £17·52 − £1·40
19. 3593 km + 298 km
20. 1329 km − 405 km

I can describe the patterns in sequences.

Example 1
460 − 10 = 450
460 − 20 = 440
460 − 30 = 430
and so on

Example 2
13 + 5 = 18
13 + 15 = 28
13 + 25 = 38
and so on

Example 3
5 + 3 = 8
50 + 30 = 80
500 + 300 = 800

Example 4

+	2	4	6	8
1	3	5	7	9
2	4	6	8	10
3	5	7	9	11
4	6	8	10	12

Patterns
→ Add 2
↓ Add 1
↗ Add 1
↘ Add 3

A

Continue the sequences from:

1 34 − 1 = 33
34 − 2 = 32
to
34 − 9 = 25

2 36 + 10 = 46
36 + 20 = 56
to
36 + 90 = 126

3 9 − 5 = 4
19 − 5 = 14
to
99 − 5 = 94

Copy and complete as in Example 3.

4 5 + 3 = 8
50 + ☐ = ☐
500 + ☐ = ☐

5 8 − 6 = 2
☐ − ☐ = ☐
☐ − ☐ = ☐

B

1 Continue the sequence from:
12 + 7 = 19
to
12 + 97 = 109

2 Describe the pattern in your sequence.

3 Write out the sequence using multiples of 10.
120 + 70 = 190
120 + 170 = 290
and so on

4 Develop a sequence as in Example 3.
a) 6 + 7 = 13
b) 15 − 8 = 7

5 Copy and complete the square.

+	1	2	3	4
2				
4				
6				
8				

6 Describe the patterns in the square.

C

Copy and complete each square. Describe the patterns.

1

+	3	6	9
2			
4			
6			

2

+	3	7	11
2			
4			
6			

Copy and complete. Extend each square into an 8 × 8 grid.

3

+	2	4	6
5			
10			
15			

4

+	4	8	12
1			
4			
7			

I can multiply one and two-digit numbers by 10 and 100 and one-digit numbers by multiples of 10.

Examples

$6 \times 10 = 60$

$62 \times 10 = 620$

$3 \times 100 = 300$

$35 \times 100 = 3500$

$70 \div 10 = 7$

$740 \div 10 = 74$

$5 \times 30 = 5 \times 3 \times 10$
$= 15 \times 10$
$= 150$

A

Work out

1. 3×10
2. 8×10
3. 6×10
4. 2×10

5. 7×10
6. 5×10
7. 9×10
8. 4×10

9. 18×10
10. 21×10
11. 45×10
12. 76×10

13. 34×10
14. 52×10
15. 89×10
16. 63×10

Copy and complete these multiplication tables.

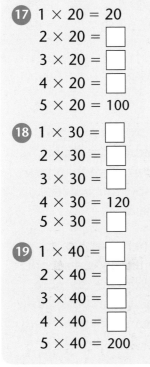

17. $1 \times 20 = 20$
$2 \times 20 = \square$
$3 \times 20 = \square$
$4 \times 20 = \square$
$5 \times 20 = 100$

18. $1 \times 30 = \square$
$2 \times 30 = \square$
$3 \times 30 = \square$
$4 \times 30 = 120$
$5 \times 30 = \square$

19. $1 \times 40 = \square$
$2 \times 40 = \square$
$3 \times 40 = \square$
$4 \times 40 = \square$
$5 \times 40 = 200$

B

Copy and complete.

1. $\square \times 10 = 320$
2. $\square \times 10 = 190$
3. $\square \times 10 = 600$
4. $\square \times 10 = 450$

5. $\square \div 10 = 23$
6. $\square \div 10 = 56$
7. $\square \div 10 = 84$
8. $\square \div 10 = 70$

9. $4 \times 100 = \square$
10. $6 \times 100 = \square$
11. $\square \times 100 = 300$
12. $\square \times 100 = 1000$

Work out

13. 50×3
14. 40×5
15. 60×4
16. 30×6

17. 90×2
18. 20×7
19. 80×3
20. 70×5

Copy and complete.

21. $120 \div 20 = \square$
22. $160 \div 4 = \square$
23. $250 \div \square = 5$
24. $350 \div \square = 50$

C

How many 10ps make:

1. £2
2. £15
3. £10
4. £9

5. £31
6. £70
7. £100
8. £148?

How many cms make:

9. 1 m
10. 3 m
11. 10 m
12. 7 m

13. 18 m
14. 49 m
15. 72 m
16. 100 m?

Work out

17. 8×60
18. 4×90
19. 6×80
20. 5×70

21. 7×200
22. 8×400
23. 9×600
24. 6×500

Copy and complete.

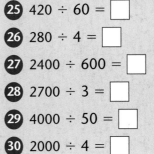

25. $420 \div 60 = \square$
26. $280 \div 4 = \square$
27. $2400 \div 600 = \square$
28. $2700 \div 3 = \square$
29. $4000 \div 50 = \square$
30. $2000 \div 4 = \square$

I can partition (split) two-digit numbers in different ways to work out subtraction and other problems.

Examples

SUBTRACTION

$$73 = 70 + 3 = 60 + 13$$
$$\underline{-36} \quad \underline{30 + 6} \quad \underline{30 + 6}$$
$$ 30 + 7 \quad\quad = 37$$

PROBLEM SOLVING   Sue and Lee share £46 but Sue gets £10 more than Lee.
How much should each get?

$$£46 = £36 + £10$$

Sue's share = £10 + (£36 ÷ 2) = £10 + £18 = £28
Lee's share = £36 ÷ 2 = £18

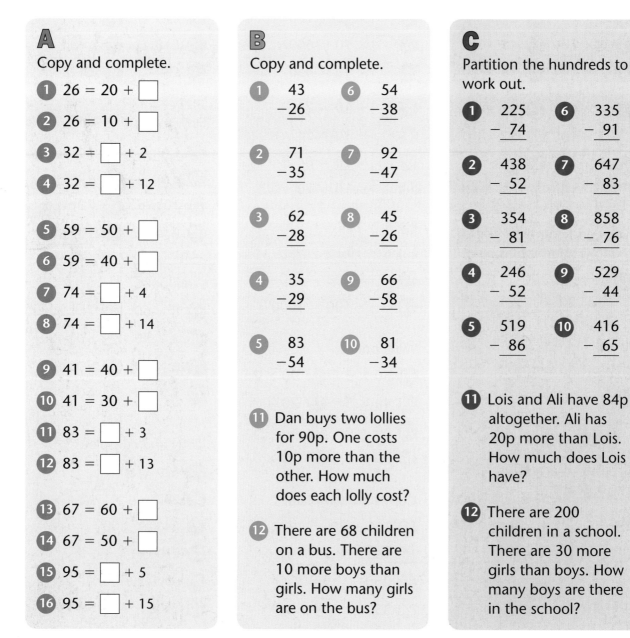

A

Copy and complete.

1 26 = 20 + ☐

2 26 = 10 + ☐

3 32 = ☐ + 2

4 32 = ☐ + 12

5 59 = 50 + ☐

6 59 = 40 + ☐

7 74 = ☐ + 4

8 74 = ☐ + 14

9 41 = 40 + ☐

10 41 = 30 + ☐

11 83 = ☐ + 3

12 83 = ☐ + 13

13 67 = 60 + ☐

14 67 = 50 + ☐

15 95 = ☐ + 5

16 95 = ☐ + 15

B

Copy and complete.

1 43 −26   6 54 −38

2 71 −35   7 92 −47

3 62 −28   8 45 −26

4 35 −29   9 66 −58

5 83 −54   10 81 −34

11 Dan buys two lollies for 90p. One costs 10p more than the other. How much does each lolly cost?

12 There are 68 children on a bus. There are 10 more boys than girls. How many girls are on the bus?

C

Partition the hundreds to work out.

1 225 − 74   6 335 − 91

2 438 − 52   7 647 − 83

3 354 − 81   8 858 − 76

4 246 − 52   9 529 − 44

5 519 − 86   10 416 − 65

11 Lois and Ali have 84p altogether. Ali has 20p more than Lois. How much does Lois have?

12 There are 200 children in a school. There are 30 more girls than boys. How many boys are there in the school?

I can add or find a difference by counting or by partitioning.

Examples

FINDING A DIFFERENCE BY COUNTING UP

USING PARTITIONING TO ADD

FINDING A DIFFERENCE BY PARTITIONING

CHECKING WITH INVERSE OPERATION

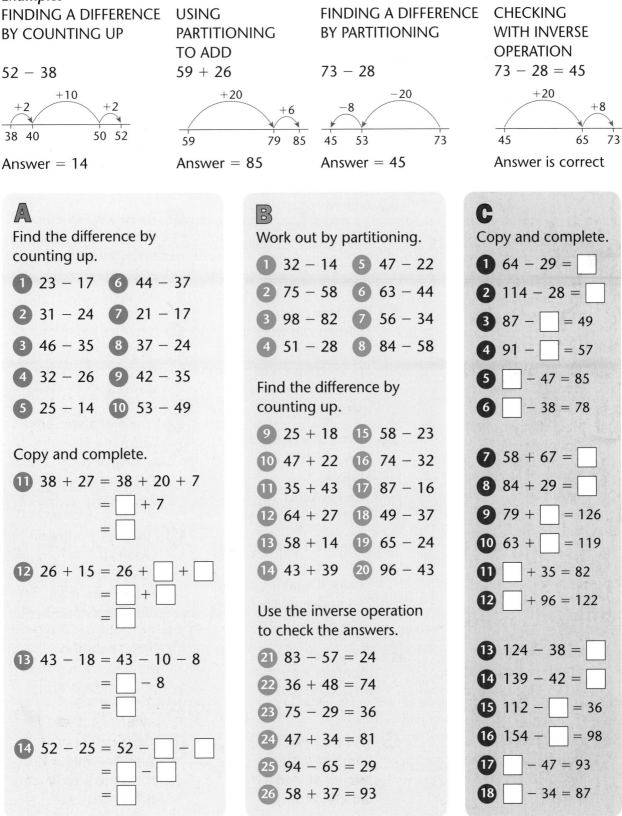

52 − 38

Answer = 14

59 + 26

Answer = 85

73 − 28

Answer = 45

73 − 28 = 45

Answer is correct

A

Find the difference by counting up.

1. 23 − 17
6. 44 − 37
2. 31 − 24
7. 21 − 17
3. 46 − 35
8. 37 − 24
4. 32 − 26
9. 42 − 35
5. 25 − 14
10. 53 − 49

Copy and complete.

11. 38 + 27 = 38 + 20 + 7
= ☐ + 7
= ☐

12. 26 + 15 = 26 + ☐ + ☐
= ☐ + ☐
= ☐

13. 43 − 18 = 43 − 10 − 8
= ☐ − 8
= ☐

14. 52 − 25 = 52 − ☐ − ☐
= ☐ − ☐
= ☐

B

Work out by partitioning.

1. 32 − 14
5. 47 − 22
2. 75 − 58
6. 63 − 44
3. 98 − 82
7. 56 − 34
4. 51 − 28
8. 84 − 58

Find the difference by counting up.

9. 25 + 18
15. 58 − 23
10. 47 + 22
16. 74 − 32
11. 35 + 43
17. 87 − 16
12. 64 + 27
18. 49 − 37
13. 58 + 14
19. 65 − 24
14. 43 + 39
20. 96 − 43

Use the inverse operation to check the answers.

21. 83 − 57 = 24
22. 36 + 48 = 74
23. 75 − 29 = 36
24. 47 + 34 = 81
25. 94 − 65 = 29
26. 58 + 37 = 93

C

Copy and complete.

1. 64 − 29 = ☐
2. 114 − 28 = ☐
3. 87 − ☐ = 49
4. 91 − ☐ = 57
5. ☐ − 47 = 85
6. ☐ − 38 = 78

7. 58 + 67 = ☐
8. 84 + 29 = ☐
9. 79 + ☐ = 126
10. 63 + ☐ = 119
11. ☐ + 35 = 82
12. ☐ + 96 = 122

13. 124 − 38 = ☐
14. 139 − 42 = ☐
15. 112 − ☐ = 36
16. 154 − ☐ = 98
17. ☐ − 47 = 93
18. ☐ − 34 = 87

I can solve puzzles and problems.

A

Find the cost of:

1. 5 sweets at 5p each
2. 2 bananas at 30p each.

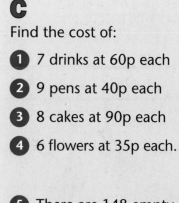

3. A baker makes 47 cakes. Five cakes can fit into one box. How many boxes are needed?
4. A teacher needs 32 pencils. There are 10 pencils in each box. How many boxes does he need?
5. I think of a number. I double it. The answer is 12. What is my number?
6. I think of a number. I halve it. The answer is 8. What is my number?
7. Find a pair of numbers which add up to 10 and have a difference of 2.
8. Find a pair of numbers which add up to 15 and have a difference of 5.

B

Find the cost of:

1. 6 stamps at 30p each
2. 4 lollies at 70p each
3. 8 apples at 20p each
4. 5 toys at 80p each.
5. A tennis coach has 42 tennis balls. Each box holds four balls. How many boxes does he need?
6. No more than 3 children can work at any one mat. There are 26 children in the PE lesson. How many mats are needed?
7. I think of a number. I double it. I take 4. The answer is 10. What is my number?
8. I think of a number. I halve it. I halve it again. The answer is 15. What is my number?
9. Find a pair of numbers with a total of 30 and a difference of 8.
10. Find a pair of numbers with a total of 40 and a difference of 12.

C

Find the cost of:

1. 7 drinks at 60p each
2. 9 pens at 40p each
3. 8 cakes at 90p each
4. 6 flowers at 35p each.
5. There are 148 empty bottles. Each crate holds 20 bottles. How many crates are needed?
6. A farmer has 80 eggs. Each box holds 6 eggs. How many boxes does he need?
7. I think of a number. I add 16. I multiply by 3. The answer is 90. What is my number?
8. I think of a number. I halve it. I take 25. The answer is 50. What is my number?
9. Find a pair of numbers with a sum of 11 and a product of 24.
10. Find a pair of numbers with a sum of 17 and a product of 60.

I can solve number problems and puzzles.

A

1. 1 and 6 scores 7. Find two other ways of scoring 7 when you roll two dice.

2. If you roll two dice what is:
   a) the highest possible score
   b) the lowest possible score?

3. If you roll two dice how many different ways can you score:
   a) 10   c) 3
   b) 6   d) 8?

4. Gina has 2ps, 5ps and 10ps only. How many different ways can she make:
   a) 20p
   b) 21p?

5. Find 5 ways of making 13 by adding 3 odd numbers.

6. Find 4 ways of making 14 by adding 3 even numbers.

B

1. 6, 5 and 1 scores 12. Find five other ways of scoring 12 when you roll three dice.

2. If you roll three dice what is the highest possible score?

3. Find four different ways of scoring 14 with three dice.

4. If you roll three dice how many different ways can you score?
   a) 16   c) 15
   b) 11   d) 13?

5. Glen has 5ps, 10ps and 20ps only. Find all the different ways he can make:
   a) 40p
   b) 55p?

6. Three children have a total of 23 crayons. Each child has a different odd number of crayons. How many crayons does each child have. Find all the different ways you can do it.

C

1. If you roll two dice and multiply the numbers, the highest possible score is 36 (6 × 6). Which numbers below 36 is it impossible to score?

2. If you roll three dice and multiply you could score 100 in one way only.
   4 × 5 × 5 = 100
   Find two different ways of scoring 20.

3. Rolling three dice find one way of scoring:
   a) 80   c) 32
   b) 216   d) 75.

4. Rolling three dice find two ways of scoring:
   a) 36   c) 48
   b) 60   d) 18.

5. There are 28 children in a class. They are told to sort themselves into three groups. Each group must have an even number but can otherwise be of any size.
   Find all the different ways the class can sort themselves into three groups.

I can use addition and subtraction facts and make patterns of linked calculations.

Example 1
13 + 5 = 18
13 + 15 = 28
13 + 25 = 38
and so on

Example 2
4 + 8 = 12
40 + 80 = 120
400 + 800 = 1200

Example 3

+	2	4	6	8
1	3	5	7	9
2	4	6	8	10
3	5	7	9	11
4	6	8	10	12

PATTERNS
Down — Add 1
Across — Add 2
Diagonal ↗ — Add 1
Diagonal ↘ — Add 3

A

Find four pairs of numbers which make each target number.

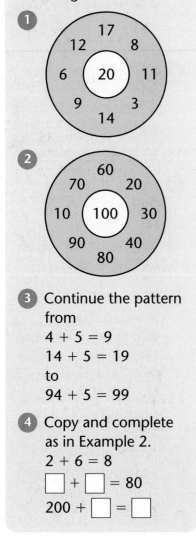

1. (circle with 20 in centre; surrounding numbers 17, 12, 8, 6, 11, 9, 3, 14)

2. (circle with 100 in centre; surrounding numbers 60, 70, 20, 10, 30, 90, 40, 80)

3. Continue the pattern from
4 + 5 = 9
14 + 5 = 19
to
94 + 5 = 99

4. Copy and complete as in Example 2.
2 + 6 = 8
☐ + ☐ = 80
200 + ☐ = ☐

B

Write the answers only.

1. 9 + 8
2. 7 + 6
3. 8 + 7
4. 9 + 4

5. 12 + 7
6. 8 + 6
7. 14 − 8
8. 20 − 7

9. 18 − 9
10. 13 − 5
11. 16 − 9
12. 17 − 8

13. 70 + 90
14. 130 + 50
15. 90 + 60
16. 80 + 80

17. 140 + 60
18. 90 + 50
19. 150 − 70
20. 200 − 140

21. 140 − 70
22. 190 − 120
23. 120 − 80
24. 170 − 90

25. Continue the pattern from
92 − 7 = 85
to
92 − 87 = 5

Develop a pattern as in Example 2.

26. 17 − 9 = 8
27. 6 + 9 = 15

C

Copy and complete.

1. 50 + ☐ = 140
2. 90 + ☐ = 160
3. 60 + ☐ = 140
4. 80 + ☐ = 170

5. 110 + ☐ = 180
6. 70 + ☐ = 150
7. 130 − ☐ = 60
8. 160 − ☐ = 80

9. 200 − ☐ = 120
10. 140 − ☐ = 50
11. 170 − ☐ = 110
12. 190 − ☐ = 130

13. Copy and complete. Describe the patterns.

+	1	4	7	10
1				
4				
7				
10				

I can add or subtract a multiple or a near-multiple of 10 and calculate near doubles.

Examples

53 + 30

53   63   73   83

Answer = 83

48 − 19

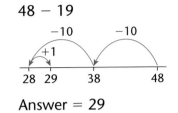

28 29   38   48

Answer = 29

35 + 37 = Double 35 + 2
        = 70 + 2
        = 72

A

Work out

1. 82 + 10   7. 59 − 10
2. 67 + 10   8. 81 − 10
3. 23 + 10   9. 74 − 10
4. 18 + 10   10. 35 − 10
5. 71 + 10   11. 93 − 10
6. 46 + 10   12. 37 − 10

13. 38 + 9   19. 76 − 9
14. 46 + 11   20. 34 − 11
15. 22 + 9   21. 47 − 9
16. 53 + 11   22. 58 − 11
17. 65 + 9   23. 63 − 9
18. 28 + 11   24. 42 − 11

25. 5 + 6   31. 30 + 29
26. 11 + 10   32. 8 + 9
27. 6 + 7   33. 11 + 12
28. 12 + 13   34. 40 + 41
29. 8 + 7   35. 15 + 16
30. 14 + 13   36. 20 + 22

B

Work out

1. 27 + 20   7. 59 − 30
2. 51 + 30   8. 96 − 50
3. 35 + 20   9. 73 − 40
4. 94 + 50   10. 132 − 20
5. 78 + 40   11. 115 − 30
6. 82 + 20   12. 128 − 60

13. 59 + 19   19. 72 − 29
14. 84 + 29   20. 45 − 19
15. 43 + 19   21. 88 − 29
16. 67 + 31   22. 39 − 21
17. 51 + 21   23. 83 − 31
18. 25 + 31   24. 66 − 21

25. 25 + 26   31. 60 + 70
26. 16 + 18   32. 18 + 20
27. 70 + 80   33. 16 + 14
28. 55 + 53   34. 80 + 70
29. 90 + 80   35. 65 + 66
30. 35 + 34   36. 19 + 17

C

Copy and complete.

1. 282 + ☐ = 332
2. 496 + ☐ = 566
3. 357 + ☐ = 437
4. 323 − ☐ = 283
5. 239 − ☐ = 179
6. 845 − ☐ = 755

7. ☐ + 41 = 93
8. ☐ − 59 = 45
9. ☐ + 49 = 116
10. ☐ − 51 = 84
11. ☐ + 62 = 145
12. ☐ − 38 = 72

Work out

13. 460 + 460
14. 290 + 290
15. 370 + 370
16. 480 + 480
17. 390 + 390
18. 280 + 280

I can quickly recall and use the multiplication facts for 2, 5 and 10.

A

Work out

1. 6×2
2. 9×2
3. 1×2
4. 8×2

5. 8×5
6. 0×5
7. 7×5
8. 6×5

9. 10×10
10. 7×10
11. 9×10
12. 8×10

13. $8 \div 2$
14. $14 \div 2$
15. $20 \div 2$
16. $18 \div 2$

17. $50 \div 5$
18. $25 \div 5$
19. $45 \div 5$
20. $30 \div 5$

21. $30 \div 10$
22. $10 \div 10$
23. $90 \div 10$
24. $60 \div 10$

B

Copy and complete.

1. $\square \times 2 = 8$
2. $\square \times 5 = 25$
3. $8 \times \square = 80$
4. $8 \times \square = 16$

5. $\square \times 5 = 0$
6. $\square \times 10 = 60$
7. $6 \times \square = 12$
8. $10 \times \square = 50$

9. $\square \times 10 = 90$
10. $\square \times 2 = 2$
11. $8 \times \square = 40$
12. $3 \times \square = 3$

13. $\square \div 5 = 6$
14. $\square \div 10 = 7$
15. $10 \div \square = 5$
16. $10 \div \square = 2$

17. $\square \div 10 = 4$
18. $\square \div 2 = 9$
19. $45 \div \square = 9$
20. $100 \div \square = 10$

21. $\square \div 2 = 7$
22. $\square \div 5 = 7$
23. $10 \div \square = 1$
24. $20 \div \square = 10$

C

Work out the brackets first.
Write the answers only.

1. $(3 \times 2) + (5 \times 5)$
2. $(6 \times 10) + (7 \times 2)$
3. $(8 \times 5) + (8 \times 10)$
4. $(9 \times 10) + (2 \times 5)$

5. $(5 \times 2) + (3 \times 10)$
6. $(10 \times 5) + (9 \times 2)$
7. $(9 \times 5) - (4 \times 2)$
8. $(5 \times 10) - (4 \times 5)$

9. $(7 \times 10) - (10 \times 2)$
10. $(4 \times 10) - (7 \times 5)$
11. $(6 \times 5) - (6 \times 2)$
12. $(10 \times 10) - (8 \times 2)$

Copy and complete the
multiplication squares.

13.

$\times$	2	5	10
7	14		70
8			
9			

14.

$\times$			
5	20		
10		60	
2			18

I can use my knowledge of the three times table to solve missing number problems.

A

Work out

1. 2×3
2. 6×3
3. 8×3
4. 1×3

5. 5×3
6. 10×3
7. 3×3
8. 7×3

9. 0×3
10. 9×3
11. 4×3
12. 11×3

13. $9 \div 3$
14. $30 \div 3$
15. $18 \div 3$
16. $3 \div 3$

17. $24 \div 3$
18. $15 \div 3$
19. $27 \div 3$
20. $6 \div 3$

21. $21 \div 3$
22. $33 \div 3$
23. $12 \div 3$
24. $36 \div 3$

B

Copy and complete.

1. $\square \times 3 = 12$
2. $\square \times 3 = 21$
3. $\square \div 3 = 3$
4. $\square \div 3 = 10$

5. $\square \times 3 = 0$
6. $\square \times 3 = 18$
7. $\square \div 3 = 2$
8. $\square \div 3 = 4$

9. $\square \times 3 = 15$
10. $\square \times 3 = 27$
11. $\square \div 3 = 1$
12. $\square \div 3 = 8$

13. $\square \times 3 = 6$
14. $\square \times 3 = 30$
15. $\square \div 3 = 7$
16. $\square \div 3 = 5$

17. $\square \times 3 = 9$
18. $\square \times 3 = 24$
19. $\square \div 3 = 6$
20. $\square \div 3 = 9$

21. Three silver stars wins one gold star. How many gold stars would you win with:
    a) 21 silver stars
    b) 60 silver stars
    c) 42 silver stars?

C

Work out

1. 20×3
2. 70×3
3. 50×3
4. 80×3
5. 30×3
6. 60×3
7. 90×3
8. 40×3
9. $300 \div 3$
10. $150 \div 3$
11. $240 \div 3$
12. $180 \div 3$
13. $270 \div 3$
14. $60 \div 3$
15. $210 \div 3$
16. $120 \div 3$

Work out by multiplying by 3 and doubling.

17. 5×6
18. 8×6
19. 3×6
20. 6×6
21. 20×6
22. 90×6
23. 40×6
24. 70×6

Work out by halving and dividing by 3.

25. $12 \div 6$
26. $36 \div 6$
27. $24 \div 6$
28. $54 \div 6$
29. $30 \div 6$
30. $42 \div 6$
31. $18 \div 6$
32. $48 \div 6$

33. There are six eggs in each box. How many eggs are there in:
    a) 8 boxes
    b) 50 boxes
    c) 35 boxes?

I can use my knowledge of the four times table to solve missing number problems.

A

Work out

1. 5×4
2. 2×4
3. 7×4
4. 0×4

5. 10×4
6. 3×4
7. 8×4
8. 11×4

9. 6×4
10. 4×4
11. 9×4
12. 12×4

13. $8 \div 4$
14. $28 \div 4$
15. $20 \div 4$
16. $36 \div 4$

17. $12 \div 4$
18. $40 \div 4$
19. $24 \div 4$
20. $4 \div 4$

21. $48 \div 4$
22. $32 \div 4$
23. $16 \div 4$
24. $44 \div 4$

B

Copy and complete.

1. $\square \times 4 = 40$
2. $\square \times 4 = 20$
3. $\square \div 4 = 3$
4. $\square \div 4 = 8$

5. $\square \times 4 = 32$
6. $\square \times 4 = 16$
7. $\square \div 4 = 2$
8. $\square \div 4 = 6$

9. $\square \times 4 = 28$
10. $\square \times 4 = 12$
11. $\square \div 4 = 5$
12. $\square \div 4 = 10$

13. $\square \times 4 = 36$
14. $\square \times 4 = 8$
15. $\square \div 4 = 1$
16. $\square \div 4 = 7$

17. $\square \times 4 = 0$
18. $\square \times 4 = 24$
19. $\square \div 4 = 4$
20. $\square \div 4 = 9$

21. There are four wheels on each car. How many wheels are needed for:
    a) 7 cars
    b) 15 cars
    c) 40 cars?

C

Work out

1. 3×4
2. 7×4
3. 4×4
4. 9×4

5. 2×4
6. 6×4
7. 5×4
8. 8×4

9. $160 \div 4$
10. $240 \div 4$
11. $400 \div 4$
12. $280 \div 4$

13. $200 \div 4$
14. $320 \div 4$
15. $120 \div 4$
16. $360 \div 4$

Work out by multiplying by 4 and doubling.

17. 4×8
18. 6×8
19. 2×8
20. 9×8

21. 50×8
22. 80×8
23. 30×8
24. 70×8

Work out by halving and dividing by 4.

25. $40 \div 8$
26. $64 \div 8$
27. $16 \div 8$
28. $72 \div 8$

29. $32 \div 8$
30. $48 \div 8$
31. $24 \div 8$
32. $56 \div 8$

33. There are eight sweets in each packet. How many packets can be made from:
    a) 88 sweets
    b) 120 sweets
    c) 200 sweets?

I can use my knowledge of the six times table to solve missing number problems.

A
Work out
1. 4×6
2. 10×6
3. 1×6
4. 7×6
5. 5×6
6. 2×6
7. 0×6
8. 8×6
9. 3×6
10. 6×6
11. 9×6
12. 12×6
13. $12 \div 6$
14. $30 \div 6$
15. $60 \div 6$
16. $42 \div 6$
17. $6 \div 6$
18. $66 \div 6$
19. $24 \div 6$
20. $48 \div 6$
21. $18 \div 6$
22. $0 \div 6$
23. $36 \div 6$
24. $54 \div 6$

B
Copy and complete.
1. $\square \times 6 = 12$
2. $\square \times 6 = 48$
3. $\square \div 6 = 5$
4. $\square \div 6 = 9$
5. $\square \times 6 = 60$
6. $\square \times 6 = 18$
7. $\square \div 6 = 7$
8. $\square \div 6 = 4$
9. $\square \times 6 = 36$
10. $\square \times 6 = 54$
11. $\square \div 6 = 2$
12. $\square \div 6 = 10$
13. $\square \times 6 = 6$
14. $\square \times 6 = 30$
15. $\square \div 6 = 6$
16. $\square \div 6 = 12$
17. $\square \times 6 = 42$
18. $\square \times 6 = 24$
19. $\square \div 6 = 3$
20. $\square \div 6 = 8$
21. There are six cakes in each box. How many cakes are there in:
    a) 9 boxes
    b) 12 boxes
    c) 20 boxes?

C
Work out
1. 40×6
2. 60×6
3. 90×6
4. 30×6
5. 50×6
6. 80×6
7. 20×6
8. 70×6
9. $180 \div 6$
10. $540 \div 6$
11. $300 \div 6$
12. $420 \div 6$
13. $120 \div 6$
14. $360 \div 6$
15. $480 \div 6$
16. $240 \div 6$

Work out by multiplying by 6 and doubling.
17. 5×12
18. 6×12
19. 2×12
20. 8×12
21. 4×12
22. 7×12
23. 3×12
24. 9×12

Work out by halving and dividing by 6.
25. $84 \div 12$
26. $24 \div 12$
27. $108 \div 12$
28. $60 \div 12$
29. $36 \div 12$
30. $96 \div 12$
31. $72 \div 12$
32. $48 \div 12$
33. There are twelve months in each year. How many months are:
    a) 6 years
    b) 50 years
    c) 21 years?

I can use my knowledge of multiplication and division to solve and make up word problems.

Examples

One bar of chocolate costs 50p.
How much do 4 bars cost?
50p × 4 = 200p
Four bars cost £2.

There are six rolls in each packet.
How many packets can be made from 18 rolls?
18 ÷ 6 = 3
3 packets can be made from 18 rolls.

A

1. One drink costs 50p. What do five drinks cost?

2. Forty grapes are shared by 10 children. How many grapes does each child have?

3. There are two ladybirds on each leaf. How many ladybirds are there on seven leaves?

4. Five sweets cost 45p. What does one sweet cost?

Make up a problem to match each number sentence.

5. 20 × 2 = 40

6. 8 × 10 = 80

7. 15 ÷ 5 = 3

8. 18 ÷ 2 = 9

B

1. Andy makes 8 triangles. How many straws does he use?

2. There are 4 cakes in one box. How many cakes are there in 30 boxes?

3. Four children sit at each table. There are 24 children in the class. How many tables are needed?

4. Three packets of stickers cost £1·50. What does one packet cost?

5. There are six eggs in each box. How many boxes are needed for 54 eggs?

Make up a story to match each number sentence.

6. 7 × 3 = 21

7. 20 × 6 = 120

8. 32 ÷ 4 = 8

9. 180 ÷ 3 = 60

C

1. How many hours is 360 minutes?

2. One theatre ticket costs £14. What do three tickets cost?

3. There are 32 children in each class. There are 6 classes in the school. How many children are there in the school?

4. The distance around the edge of a square playground is 100 metres. How long is one side?

5. Eight biscuits weigh 160 g altogether. What does one biscuit weigh?

Make up a story to match each number sentence.

6. 9 × 8 = 72

7. 84 ÷ 6 = 14

8. 140 ÷ 7 = 20

9. 4 × 12 = 48

I can find different ways of folding squares and rectangles into halves and quarters.

A

This diagram shows one way of folding a square piece of paper into two equal pieces or two halves.

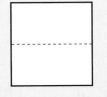

1 Use a square piece of paper. Find different ways of folding the paper into two equal halves.

2 Show all the different ways you have found in diagrams like the one above.

3 Find different ways of folding a rectangle into halves. Show the ways you have found in diagrams.

4

Look at the shape. Write $\frac{1}{2}$, $\frac{1}{4}$ or $\frac{3}{4}$ in each box.

a) ☐ of the shape is yellow

b) ☐ of the shape is orange

c) ☐ of the shape is red

d) ☐ of the shape is not red

B

1 Use a square piece of paper. Find different ways of folding the paper into four equal pieces or four quarters.

2 Show all the different ways you have found in diagrams.

3 Investigate folding a rectangular piece of paper into quarters. Record your different ways in diagrams.

4 Which of these shapes could be folded:

a) into halves

b) into quarters?

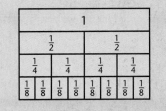

5

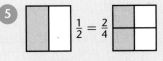

$\frac{1}{2} = \frac{2}{4}$

Find other ways of showing that $\frac{1}{2} = \frac{2}{4}$ using squares or rectangles.

C

1 Find different ways of folding a square or rectangular piece of paper into eight equal pieces or 8 eighths.

2 Show all the different ways you have found in diagrams.

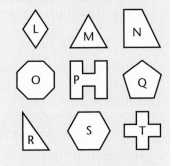

Use the fractions chart to copy and complete by filling in the box.

3 $1 = \frac{\square}{2}$ **7** $\frac{1}{2} = \frac{\square}{8}$

4 $\frac{1}{4} = \frac{\square}{8}$ **8** $\frac{2}{4} = \frac{\square}{8}$

5 $\frac{1}{2} = \frac{\square}{4}$ **9** $1 = \frac{\square}{4}$

6 $1 = \frac{\square}{8}$ **10** $\frac{3}{4} = \frac{\square}{8}$

11 Make a fraction chart like the one above by folding a rectangular piece of paper.

12 Which of the shapes L to T in Section B could be folded into eighths?

Find different ways of showing:

13 $\frac{1}{4} = \frac{2}{8}$ **14** $\frac{3}{4} = \frac{6}{8}$

I can recognise line symmetry in 2-D shapes and complete a partly drawn symmetrical shape.

A shape is symmetrical if half of its shape matches the other half exactly. The line separating the two halves is the line of symmetry or mirror line.

Examples
One line of symmetry

Two lines of symmetry

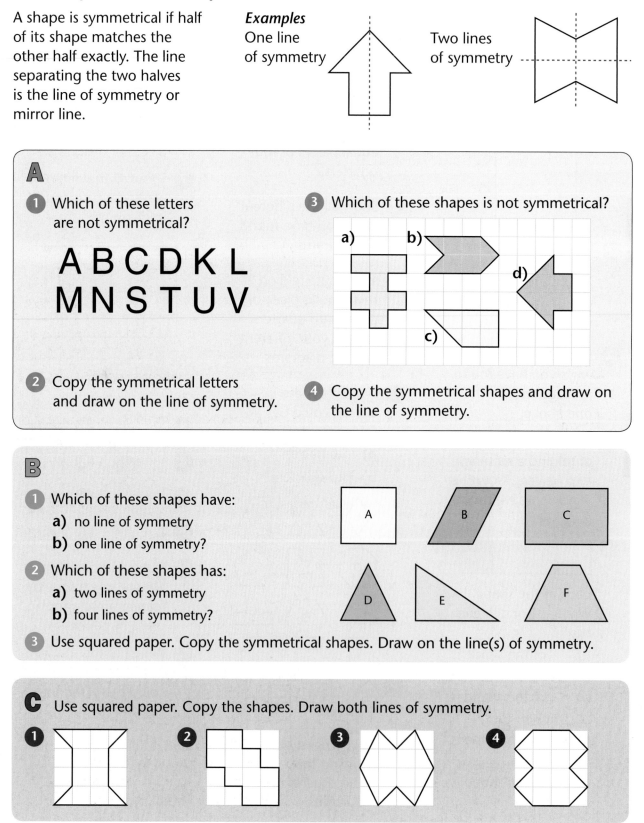

A

1 Which of these letters are not symmetrical?

A B C D K L M N S T U V

2 Copy the symmetrical letters and draw on the line of symmetry.

3 Which of these shapes is not symmetrical?

a)   b)   d)

c)

4 Copy the symmetrical shapes and draw on the line of symmetry.

B

1 Which of these shapes have:
  a) no line of symmetry
  b) one line of symmetry?

2 Which of these shapes has:
  a) two lines of symmetry
  b) four lines of symmetry?

A   B   C

D   E   F

3 Use squared paper. Copy the symmetrical shapes. Draw on the line(s) of symmetry.

C Use squared paper. Copy the shapes. Draw both lines of symmetry.

1   **2**   **3**   **4**

I can make and describe 2-D shapes.

3 sides – triangle   4 sides – quadrilateral   5 sides – pentagon
                                   square   6 sides – hexagon
                                   rectangle   8 sides – octagon

A

For each of the shapes write:
a) the number of sides
b) the name of the shape.

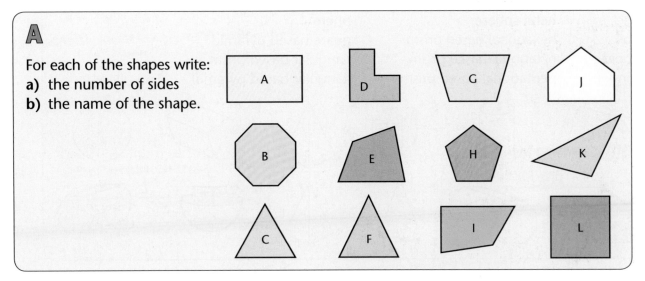

B

Write the letter and name of the above shape which is:

1 a symmetrical quadrilateral with no right angle

2 a triangle with one pair of equal sides

3 a pentagon with all its sides equal

4 a quadrilateral with a right angle which is not symmetrical.

These triangles are made on 3 × 3 grids.

5 Which of these triangles have:
a) a right angle
b) 2 equal sides
c) a line of symmetry?

6 Use squared or dotty paper.
Make some more triangles on 3 × 3 grids. Describe them.

C

Write the letters and names of all the above shapes which:

1 have more than one line of symmetry

2 are quadrilaterals and have a right angle

3 are symmetrical triangles

4 have one or more pairs of equal sides

5 have all their sides equal.

These quadrilaterals are made on 3 × 3 grids.

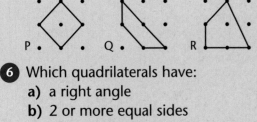

6 Which quadrilaterals have:
a) a right angle
b) 2 or more equal sides
c) a line of symmetry?

7 Use squared or dotty paper.
Make some more quadrilaterals on 3 × 3 grids. Describe them.

I can describe the features of 3-D shapes.

A

Match each of the shapes A to L with one of the names of 3-D shapes.

cone	hemi-sphere	sphere
cube	hexagonal based prism	square based pyramid
cuboid	octagonal based prism	triangular based prism
cylinder	pentagonal based prism	triangular based pyramid

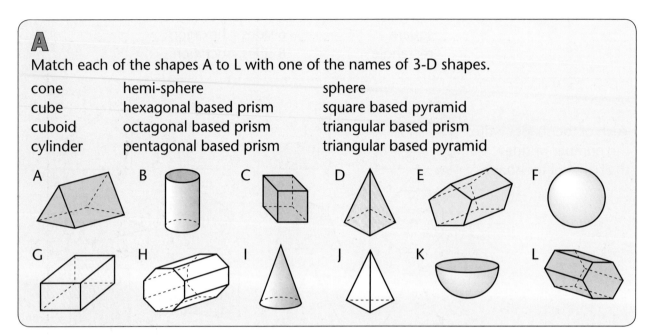

A   B   C   D   E   F

G   H   I   J   K   L

B

Look at the above shapes A to L.
Write the letter and name of each shape.

1. It has triangular faces only.

2. It has 12 vertices.

3. It is half a sphere.

4. It has 9 edges.

5. It has 6 identical faces.

6. It has 7 faces.

7. It has 2 curved edges.

8. It has 16 vertices.

How many straws would you need to build:

9. a cube

10. a square pyramid

11. a triangular pyramid

12. a cuboid?

C

Look at the above shapes A to L.

1. Which shapes have faces which only meet at a right angle?

2. Which shapes with straight edges have no faces which meet at a right angle?

3. A prism has six vertices. How many faces does it have?

4. This is the end face of a prism. How many vertices does it have?

How many straws would you need to build:

5. a triangular based prism

6. an octagonal based prism

7. a hexagonal based prism

8. a pentagonal based prism?

I can match 3-D shapes to pictures of them and build 3-D shapes from pictures.

A
Use cubes to build these shapes.

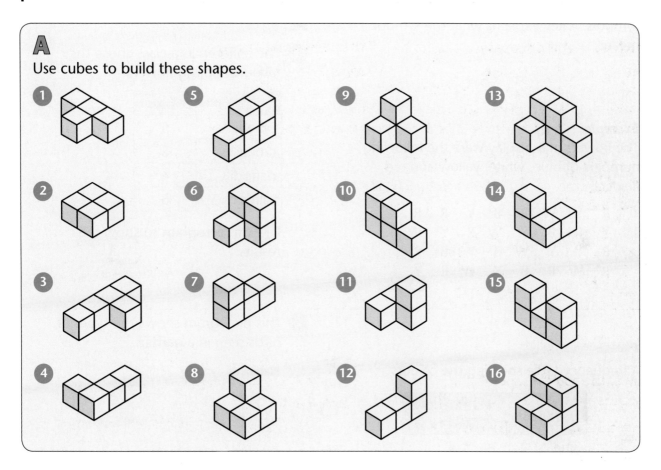

B
Without using cubes, work out how many cubes are needed to build each of the above shapes.

Example   6 cubes are needed.
(Only 5 cubes can be seen.)

C
How many more cubes are needed to turn each of the above shapes into a cuboid?

Example   2 cubes are needed.

I can make a pictogram where a symbol represents 2 units.

A pictogram shows data (information) in symbols. A key explains what the symbol means.

Example
The flowers in a display were the following numbers of blue, white, yellow and red flowers.

```
R   Y   W   R   B   Y   R   R
Y   R   B   Y   W   R   Y   W
R   Y   Y   W   R   Y   B   R
R   W   R   B   Y   W   R   Y
```

A frequency table showing the colours.

Colours	Number of flowers
Blue	4
Red	12
White	6
Yellow	10

The data in the frequency table can be displayed in a pictogram.

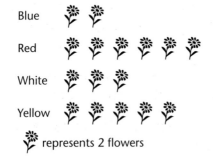

represents 2 flowers

A

① The children in a class chose their favourite spring flowers.

Flower	Votes
bluebells	5
crocuses	3
daffodils	4
tulips	6

Draw a pictogram to show the results.

② This pictogram shows the types of birds seen in a garden.

Blackbirds   ⌒ ⌒ ⌒ ⌒

Sparrows   ⌒ ⌒ ⌒ ⌒ ⌒ ⌒

Starlings   ⌒ ⌒ ⌒ ⌒ ⌒ ⌒ ⌒

Thrushes   ⌒ ⌒ ⌒

⌒ represents 1 bird

a) Which type of bird was seen most often?

b) Which type of bird was seen least often?

c) How many blackbirds were seen in the garden?

d) How many more sparrows than blackbirds were seen in the garden?

e) How many fewer thrushes than starlings were seen in the garden?

f) How many birds were seen in the garden altogether?

B

1 The children on a school trip brought these drinks.

Flavours	Number of drinks
apple	4
blackcurrant	6
cola	12
orange	10

Draw a pictogram to show the data.

This pictogram shows how the children in Class 3 come to school.

represents 2 children

2 How many children walk to school?

3 How many come by bike?

4 Which is the most common way that the children come to school?

5 Which is the least common way?

6 Which form of transport is used by 6 children?

7 How many more children walk than cycle?

8 How many fewer children come by bus than by car?

9 How many children are there in the class?

C

1 In one day a sweet shop sold these numbers of packets of chocolate, fruit, mint and toffee sweets.

```
T C F C T M C T F C
C F M T C F C M T F
M C F C T T F C M T
T F C M C T M F T C
T C F M C F T T F C
```

Make a frequency table and then draw a pictogram to show the results.

The children in Year 3 voted for how they would most like to come to school. The results are shown in the pictogram.

Balloon
Helicopter
Horseback
Limousine
Time Machine

represents 5 votes

2 Which form of transport got:
   a) 5 votes   **b)** 30 votes?

3 How many children voted for coming to school on horseback?

4 How many more children voted for a ride in a helicopter rather than in a limousine?

5 How many fewer children voted to travel in a balloon rather than by time machine?

6 Everybody had one vote only. How many children voted?

7 How would *you* like to come to school?

I can use a bar chart to find information and draw a bar chart labelled in twos.

Example
The ages of children in a basketball club.

```
10   9   8  10   9  10  11
 8  10  11   9  10   8  10
 9  10  10   8  11  10   9
10  11   9  10   8   9  10
```

A frequency table showing the ages.

Ages	No. of children
8	5
9	7
10	12
11	4

The data in the frequency table can be displayed in a bar chart.

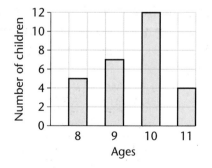

Notice:
- each axis is labelled
- the vertical axis goes up in 2s
- the bars do not touch
- the bars are of equal width.

A

This block graph shows the number of children absent from school each day in Year 3.

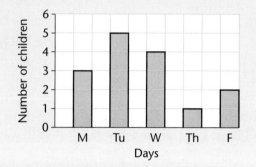

1. How many children were absent on Monday?

2. On which day were 4 children absent?

3. On which day were most children absent?

4. On which day were least children absent?

5. How many more children were absent on Wednesday than on Friday?

6. How many fewer children were absent on Monday than on Tuesday?

7. This frequency table shows how children in a class came to school on one day.

Travel Method	Number of Children
Bus	3
Bike	4
Car	5
Train	2
Walk	6

Draw a block graph to show the information.

B

This graph shows the passengers on a bus.

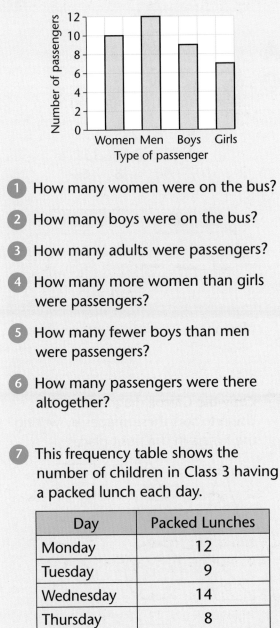

1. How many women were on the bus?

2. How many boys were on the bus?

3. How many adults were passengers?

4. How many more women than girls were passengers?

5. How many fewer boys than men were passengers?

6. How many passengers were there altogether?

7. This frequency table shows the number of children in Class 3 having a packed lunch each day.

Day	Packed Lunches
Monday	12
Tuesday	9
Wednesday	14
Thursday	8
Friday	13

Draw a bar chart labelled in twos to show the information.

8. There are 30 children in Class 3. All the other children have a school dinner. Make a frequency table and then draw a bar chart showing the number of children in Class 3 having a school dinner each day.

C

This graph shows how many children in each year group walked to school every day in January.

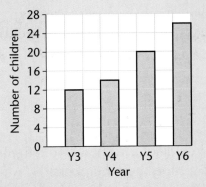

1. How many children walked to school in Year 5?

2. In which year group did 14 children walk to school?

3. How many more children walked to school in Year 6 than in Year 5?

4. How many fewer children walked to school in Year 3 than in Year 4?

5. How many children walked to school altogether?

6. Draw what you think the graph might look like in July. There are 60 children in each year.

7. The children in a school voted for the colour of their new school uniform. The frequency table shows the results.

Colour	Votes
black	30
blue	50
green	45
red	65
yellow	55

Draw a bar chart labelled in 10s to show the results.

I can place objects on a Carroll diagram.

A Carroll diagram is a way of sorting numbers, shapes or objects into groups.

Example

The Carroll diagrams show two different ways of sorting these numbers.

```
4    8    53    96
5   10    62   125
7   29    87   248
```

	even	not even
2-digit	10 62 96	29 53 87
not 2-digit	4 8 248	5 7 125

	odd	not odd
over 20	29 53 87 125	62 96 248
not over 20	5 7	4 8 10

CHARLES DODGSON

Carroll diagrams were invented in Victorian times by Charles Dodgson, a mathematician. He is better known as the author of the famous children's book, *Alice's Adventures in Wonderland*. The name Charles Dodgson however, does not appear on the cover of that book. He used a different name. Do you know what it was?

A

1. Copy the Carroll diagram.
   Use it to sort these numbers.

```
 19    6   285    27
  2   94    71   152
107   60     8    68
```

2-digit	not 2-digit

2. Copy the Carroll diagram.
   Use it to sort these shapes by writing the letters in the right places.

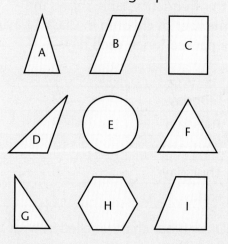

symmetrical	not symmetrical

B

1 Copy the Carroll diagram.
Use it to sort the numbers 1 to 30.

	multiples of 3	not multiples of 3
multiples of 2		
not multiples of 2		

2 Write down the next two numbers after 30 which are:

a) multiples of 2 and multiples of 3

b) not multiples of 2 but are multiples of 3.

3 Copy the Carroll diagram.
Use it sort these shapes by writing the letters in the right places.

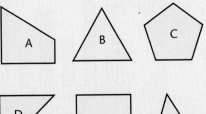
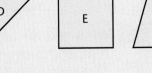

	has right angle	does not have right angle
triangles		
not triangles		

C

1 Copy the Carroll diagram.
Use it to sort the multiples of 5 to 100.

	multiples of 3	not multiples of 3
multiples of 2		
not multiples of 2		

2 Write down the next two multiples of 5 after 100 which are:

a) multiples of 2 and multiples of 3

b) not multiples of 2 but are multiples of 3.

3 Copy the Carroll diagram.
Use it to sort these shapes by writing the letters in the right places.

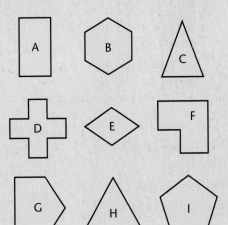

	4 sides	not 4 sides
all sides equal		
not all sides equal		

I can read the temperature on a thermometer and use a bar chart to find information.

Temperature is measured in degrees (°).
The most common scale is the Celsius scale,
on which water freezes at 0°C.
The temperature can fall below 0°C, to −1°C,
−2°C, −3°C and so on.

Examples

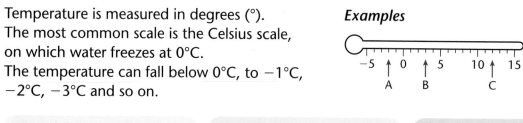

A = −2°C
B = 3°C
C = 12°C

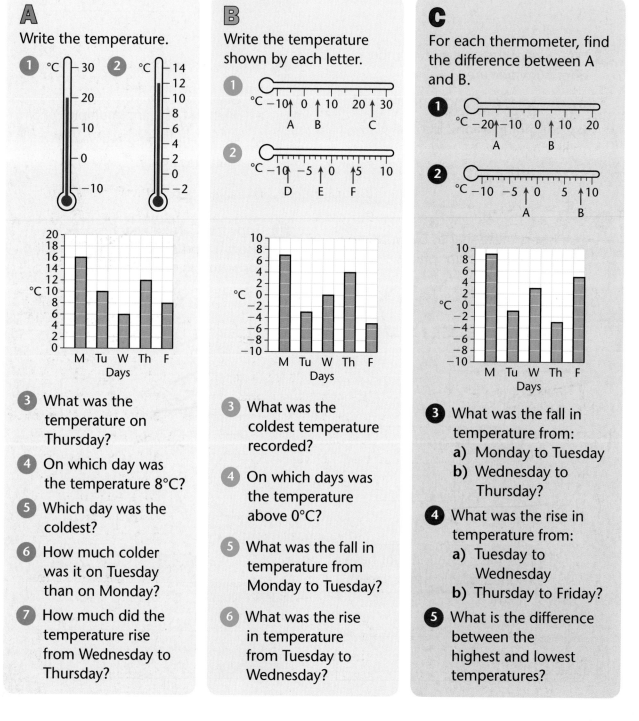

A
Write the temperature.

3 What was the temperature on Thursday?

4 On which day was the temperature 8°C?

5 Which day was the coldest?

6 How much colder was it on Tuesday than on Monday?

7 How much did the temperature rise from Wednesday to Thursday?

B
Write the temperature shown by each letter.

3 What was the coldest temperature recorded?

4 On which days was the temperature above 0°C?

5 What was the fall in temperature from Monday to Tuesday?

6 What was the rise in temperature from Tuesday to Wednesday?

C
For each thermometer, find the difference between A and B.

3 What was the fall in temperature from:
a) Monday to Tuesday
b) Wednesday to Thursday?

4 What was the rise in temperature from:
a) Tuesday to Wednesday
b) Thursday to Friday?

5 What is the difference between the highest and lowest temperatures?

I can find a difference between two measurements by counting up.

Examples

Find the difference between 47 m and 74 m?

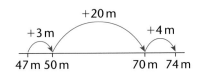

Answer *27 m*

What is the difference between 185 g and 230 g?

Answer *45 g*

A

Find the difference between:

1. £49 and £33
2. 60 g and 20 g
3. 37 kg and 24 kg
4. 58 m and 10 m

5. 24 cm and 8 cm
6. 500 ml and 100 ml
7. 63 kg and 51 kg
8. 50p and 35p.

9. The longest throw is 58 metres. The shortest is 46 m. What is the difference between the throws?

10. One plant is 72 cm tall. Another plant is 63 cm tall. What is the difference between the heights of the two plants?

11. The difference between Jock and Corey's weight is 13 kg. Corey is lighter than Jock. Corey weighs 34 kg. What does Jock weigh?

B

Find the difference between:

1. 1000 ml and 200 ml
2. 84p and 58p
3. £95 and £40
4. 65 cm and 32 cm

5. 300 ml and 120 ml
6. 98 kg and 79 kg
7. 750 g and 500 g
8. 77 km and 54 km.

9. One packet of breakfast cereal holds 675 g. Another packet holds 750 g. What is the difference between the weights of the packets?

10. The difference in price between two magazines is 24p. The cheaper one costs 55p. What does the other magazine cost?

11. The largest water butt holds 68 litres. The smallest holds 32 litres. What is the difference between the capacities of the water butts?

C

Find the difference between:

1. £5·00 and £2·99
2. 147 m and 114 m
3. 1200 g and 850 g
4. 120 km and 48 km

5. 400 ml and 175 ml
6. 108 kg and 79 kg
7. £1350 and £900
8. £2·59 and £1·80.

9. The longest golf drive was 246 metres. The shortest was 172 metres. What was the difference in length between the longest and shortest drives?

10. Adam's apple weighs 190 g. Eve's weighs 115 g. What is the difference in weight between the two apples?

11. The difference in price between two television sets is £144. The more expensive set costs £627. What does the cheaper set cost?

I can add or subtract multiples and near multiples of 10 or 100.

Examples

54 kg − 30 kg

£3·60 + £1·99

A

Work out

1. 25 m + 10 m
2. 37 m − 10 m
3. 59 ml + 10 ml
4. 42 ml − 10 ml

5. 78 cm + 10 cm
6. 78 cm + 9 cm
7. 64 kg − 10 kg
8. 64 kg − 11 kg

9. £3·20 − £1·00
10. £3·20 − 99p
11. £513 + £100
12. £513 + £102

13. Ross has £1·76. He spends 99p. How much does he have left?

14. Josie has 260 g of weights on a balance. She adds two 100 g weights. How much weight is there now on the balance?

B

Work out

1. 59 litres + 30 litres
2. 92 litres − 20 litres
3. 184 g + 50 g
4. 361 g − 40 g

5. 53 cm + 41 cm
6. 78 cm − 29 cm
7. 46p + 19p
8. £1·85 − 31p

9. 480 m + 300 m
10. 675 ml − 400 ml
11. £5·95 − £1·99
12. £3·24 + £2·99

13. Anika has 750 ml of orange juice. She fills three 200 ml glasses. How much orange juice is left?

14. Owen has 56p. Greg has 31p. How much do they have altogether?

15. A string is 95 cm long. 50 cm is cut off. How much is left?

C

Work out

1. 575 g + 60 g
2. 325 g − 30 g
3. 1235 km + 700 km
4. 2390 km − 500 km

5. £1456 + £32
6. £2372 − £49
7. 295 litres + 27 litres
8. 138 litres − 61 litres

9. £18·27 + £5·99
10. £43·65 − £2·03
11. 1951 km + 406 km
12. 3674 km − 898 km

13. Harry buys presents costing £3·50, £2·99 and £1·99. How much has he spent?

14. Going on holiday, Pam travelled 97 miles by coach to the airport. She flew 1485 miles and then had a 21 mile taxi ride to her hotel. How far had she travelled?

I can solve word problems involving multiplication and division.

Examples

A square field has sides 200 metres long. What is the length of the fence around the field?

$200\,m \times 4 = 800\,m$

Answer   *The fence is 800 m long.*

A roll of tape is 10 metres long. One fifth is used. How much is left?

$\frac{1}{5}$ of $10\,m = 10\,m \div 5$

$\qquad\qquad = 2\,m$

$10\,m - 2\,m = 8\,m$

Answer   *8 metres of tape is left.*

A

1. A watering can holds 4 litres. It can be filled 10 times from a barrel. How much water does the barrel hold?

2. A piece of wood is 60 cm long. It is sawn in half. How long is each length?

3. A box of apples weighs 6 kg. What do five boxes weigh?

4. A pile of ten dictionaries is 30 cm tall. How thick is one dictionary?

5. Claire has two ribbons. One is 40 cm long. The other is twice as long. How long is the longer ribbon?

6. A rope is 20 metres long. One quarter is cut off. How long are the two ropes?

B

1. A can of beans weighs 400 g. It makes two servings. What is one serving?

2. Rover takes 20 ml of medicine every day for six days. How much medicine does he take altogether?

3. Hugh watches one third of a 45 minute television programme and records the rest. How long is the recorded part of the programme?

4. Glasses hold 200 ml. How much drink is needed for three glasses?

5. Six eggs weigh 360 g. What does one egg weigh?

C

1. One tile is 12 cm long. What is the length of a row of eight tiles?

2. The distance around the edge of a square playground is 56 metres. How long is one side?

3. A football match lasts 90 minutes. After how many minutes do the players stop for half time?

4. A bag of flour contains 1000 g. One quarter of the bag is used. How much is left?

5. An athlete trains by running 800 metres five times. How far does she run altogether?

6. A tea cup holds 150 ml. How many cups can be filled from a 1200 ml teapot?

I can change pounds to pence and pence to pounds and I can solve problems involving money.

Examples

564p = £5·64
170p = £1·70
206p = £2·06
85p = £0·85
7p = £0·07

SCHOOL SHOP PRICES

pencil	15p	T shirt	£3·20
pen	45p	sweatshirt	£8·80
ruler	25p	PE bag	£2·50
rubber	20p	homework bag	£3·50
felt tips	80p	dictionary	£3·75

A

Change to pence.

1. £1·50
2. £1·35
3. £2·20
4. £3·75

Change to pounds and pence.

5. 165p
6. 240p
7. 130p
8. 215p

Use the above price list. Work out the cost of:

9. 2 pens
10. 2 rulers
11. 3 rubbers
12. 2 pencils
13. ruler and rubber
14. pen and pencil
15. felt tips and rubber
16. pen and ruler

How many of these items could you buy for £1·00?

17. rubbers
18. rulers
19. pens
20. pencils

B

Change to pence.

1. £7·26
2. £4·04
3. £3·72
4. £9·08

Change to pounds and pence.

5. 257p
6. 349p
7. 74p
8. 201p

Use the above price list. Work out the cost of:

9. 2 packs of felt tips
10. 2 T shirts
11. PE bag, homework bag
12. dictionary, pen
13. Three small packets of sweets cost the same as two large packets. One small packet costs 30p. What does one large packet cost?
14. What different amounts can you make choosing any 3 of these coins?

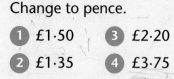

C

Find the cost of these items and the change from £10·00.

1. 5 packs of felt tips
2. sweatshirt, 6 pencils
3. homework bag, dictionary
4. 2 pens, ruler, PE bag
5. You buy a sweatshirt, a pen and one other item. You pay with a £10 note and receive 50p change. What was the other item?
6. A special offer allows you to buy two boxes of chocolates but get the second one for half price. You pay £6·75. What does one box cost?
7. Find all the different amounts you can make choosing any 3 of these coins.

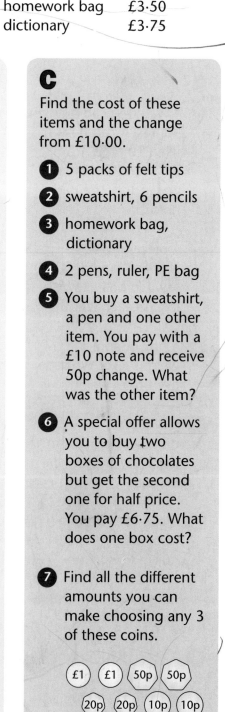

I can use my knowledge of the relationship between metric units and I can suggest suitable units to measure lengths, weights or capacities.

LENGTH
100 cm = 1 m   1000 m = 1 km
200 cm = 2 m   2000 m = 2 km
300 cm = 3 m   3000 m = 3 km
and so on   and so on

WEIGHT
1000 g = 1 kg
2000 g = 2 kg
3000 g = 3 kg
and so on

CAPACITY
1000 ml = 1 litre
2000 ml = 2 litres
3000 ml = 3 litres
and so on

A

Copy and complete.

1. 1 kg = ☐ g
2. 1 m = ☐ cm
3. 2 km = ☐ m
4. 3 litres = ☐ ml

5. 1 km = ☐ m
6. 2 litres = ☐ ml
7. 3 kg = ☐ g
8. 2 m = ☐ cm

9. 1 litre = ☐ ml
10. 3 km = ☐ m
11. 3 m = ☐ cm
12. 2 kg = ☐ g

Choose the more sensible estimate.

13. a toothbrush
    5 cm or 15 cm
14. a tea cup
    200 ml or 2 litres
15. a bag of sugar
    100 g or 1 kg
16. a beetle
    1 cm or 10 cm

B

Copy and complete.

1. $\frac{1}{2}$ m = ☐ cm
2. 5 kg = ☐ g
3. 3000 ml = ☐ litres
4. 4 km = ☐ m

5. 200 cm = ☐ m
6. 500 g = ☐ kg
7. 9000 ml = ☐ litres
8. $\frac{1}{2}$ km = ☐ m

9. 6 m = ☐ cm
10. 2000 g = ☐ kg
11. $\frac{1}{2}$ litre = ☐ ml
12. 5000 m = ☐ km

Suggest a suitable metric unit to measure:

13. a chair's height
14. a bucket's capacity
15. a book's weight
16. a running track's length
17. the capacity of a glass
18. a lawn mower's weight.

C

Copy and complete.

1. 65 cm + ☐ = 1 m
2. 350 g + ☐ = 1 kg
3. 850 ml + ☐ = 1 litre
4. 550 m + ☐ = 1 km

5. 15 cm + ☐ = 1 m
6. 450 g + ☐ = 1 kg
7. 750 ml + ☐ = 1 litre
8. 950 m + ☐ = 1 km

9. 25 cm + ☐ = 1 m
10. 250 g + ☐ = 1 kg
11. 50 ml + ☐ = 1 litre
12. 150 m + ☐ = 1 km

Copy the sentences, choosing the most sensible estimate.

13. A door is (1 m, 2 m, 10 cm) tall.
14. A washing up bowl holds (500 ml, 5 litres, 50 litres).
15. A baby weighs (30 g, 300 g, 3 kg).
16. A garden is (20 m, 200 m, 2 km) long.

I can measure or draw lines accurately to the nearest half centimetre.

Start measuring from 0,
not from the end of the ruler,
and read the scale.

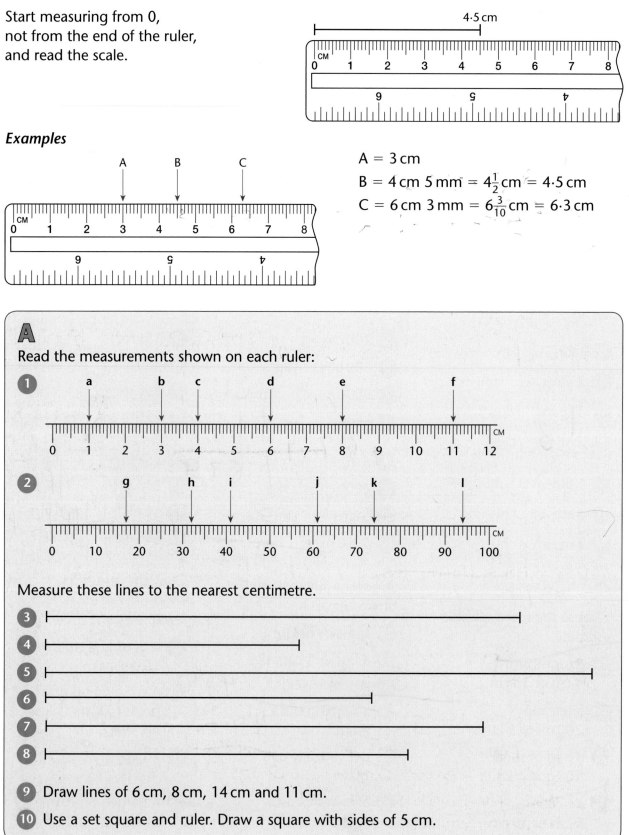

Examples

A = 3 cm

B = 4 cm 5 mm = $4\frac{1}{2}$ cm = 4·5 cm

C = 6 cm 3 mm = $6\frac{3}{10}$ cm = 6·3 cm

A

Read the measurements shown on each ruler:

1

2

Measure these lines to the nearest centimetre.

3

4

5

6

7

8

9 Draw lines of 6 cm, 8 cm, 14 cm and 11 cm.

10 Use a set square and ruler. Draw a square with sides of 5 cm.

B

Read the measurements shown on each ruler:

①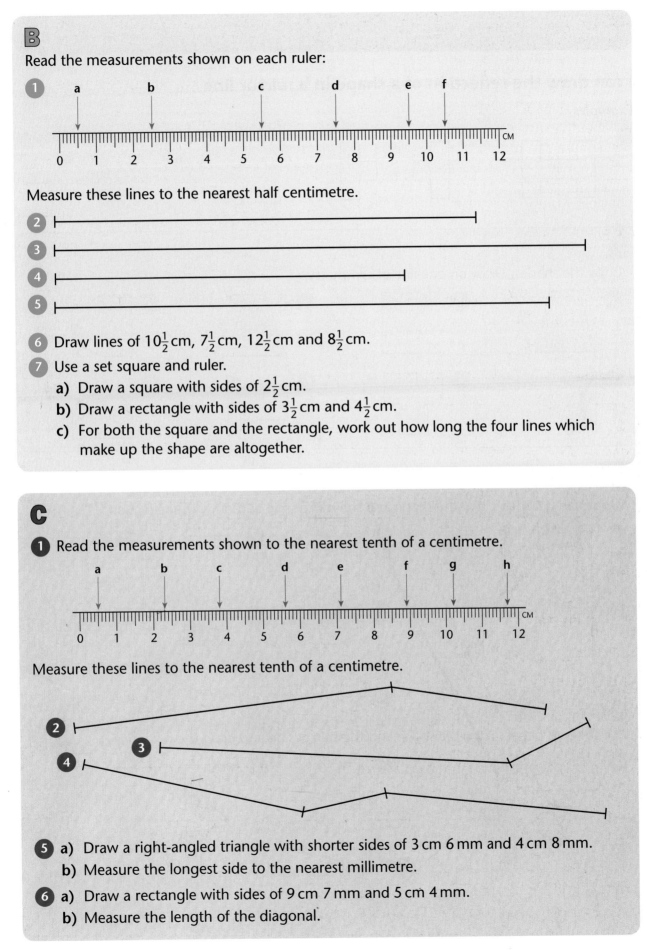

Measure these lines to the nearest half centimetre.

②

③

④

⑤

⑥ Draw lines of $10\frac{1}{2}$ cm, $7\frac{1}{2}$ cm, $12\frac{1}{2}$ cm and $8\frac{1}{2}$ cm.

⑦ Use a set square and ruler.
   a) Draw a square with sides of $2\frac{1}{2}$ cm.
   b) Draw a rectangle with sides of $3\frac{1}{2}$ cm and $4\frac{1}{2}$ cm.
   c) For both the square and the rectangle, work out how long the four lines which make up the shape are altogether.

C

① Read the measurements shown to the nearest tenth of a centimetre.

Measure these lines to the nearest tenth of a centimetre.

②

③

④

⑤ a) Draw a right-angled triangle with shorter sides of 3 cm 6 mm and 4 cm 8 mm.
   b) Measure the longest side to the nearest millimetre.

⑥ a) Draw a rectangle with sides of 9 cm 7 mm and 5 cm 4 mm.
   b) Measure the length of the diagonal.

I can draw the reflection of a shape in a mirror line.

Examples

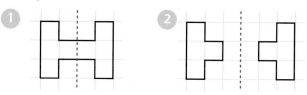

A

Copy the shapes. Draw on one line of symmetry.

B

Use squared paper. Copy the shape and the mirror line and draw the reflection.

C

Use squared paper. Copy the shape and the mirror line and draw the reflection.

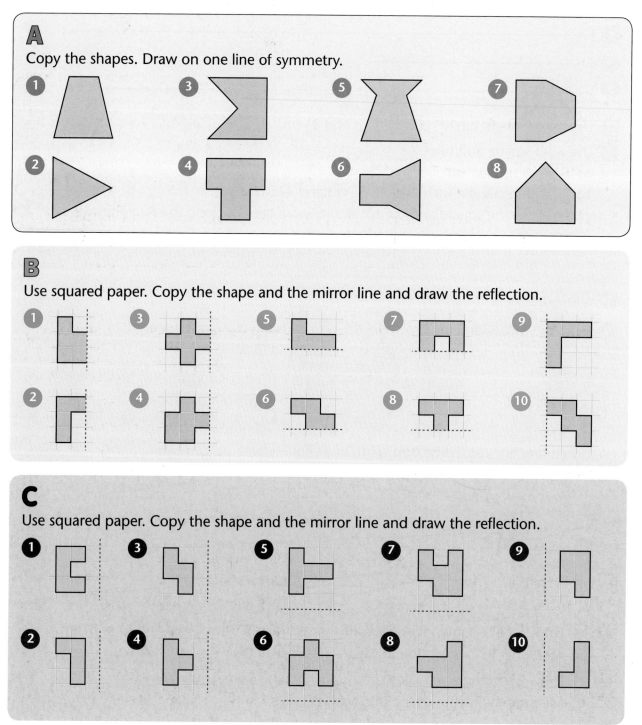

I can recognise half turns and right angles and use them to follow or give directions.

A $\frac{1}{4}$ turn is a right angle or 90°   A half turn is two quarter turns or 180°

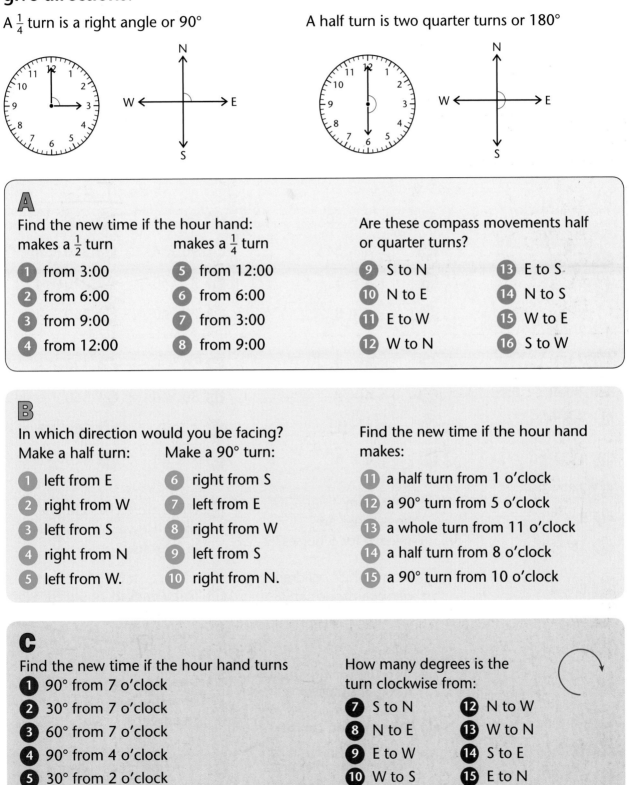

A

Find the new time if the hour hand:

makes a $\frac{1}{2}$ turn

1 from 3:00
2 from 6:00
3 from 9:00
4 from 12:00

makes a $\frac{1}{4}$ turn

5 from 12:00
6 from 6:00
7 from 3:00
8 from 9:00

Are these compass movements half or quarter turns?

9 S to N
10 N to E
11 E to W
12 W to N

13 E to S
14 N to S
15 W to E
16 S to W

B

In which direction would you be facing?

Make a half turn:

1 left from E
2 right from W
3 left from S
4 right from N
5 left from W.

Make a 90° turn:

6 right from S
7 left from E
8 right from W
9 left from S
10 right from N.

Find the new time if the hour hand makes:

11 a half turn from 1 o'clock
12 a 90° turn from 5 o'clock
13 a whole turn from 11 o'clock
14 a half turn from 8 o'clock
15 a 90° turn from 10 o'clock

C

Find the new time if the hour hand turns

1 90° from 7 o'clock
2 30° from 7 o'clock
3 60° from 7 o'clock
4 90° from 4 o'clock
5 30° from 2 o'clock
6 60° from 11 o'clock.

How many degrees is the turn clockwise from:

7 S to N
8 N to E
9 E to W
10 W to S
11 E to S

12 N to W
13 W to N
14 S to E
15 E to N
16 N to S?

I can use the multiplication facts for 3, 4 and 6 to solve problems.

A

What is

1. 10×3
2. 7×3
3. 4×3
4. 9×3

5. 5×4
6. 8×4
7. 3×4
8. 6×4

9. 2×6
10. 9×6
11. 5×6
12. 8×6

13. $15 \div 3$
14. $24 \div 3$
15. $9 \div 3$
16. $18 \div 3$

17. $8 \div 4$
18. $36 \div 4$
19. $28 \div 4$
20. $40 \div 4$

21. $24 \div 6$
22. $42 \div 6$
23. $6 \div 6$
24. $36 \div 6$

B

Copy and complete.

1. $\square \times 3 = 27$
2. $\square \times 3 = 6$
3. $\square \times 4 = 32$
4. $\square \times 4 = 16$

5. $\square \times 6 = 30$
6. $\square \times 6 = 54$
7. $\square \div 3 = 5$
8. $\square \div 3 = 8$

9. $\square \div 4 = 9$
10. $\square \div 4 = 7$
11. $\square \div 6 = 1$
12. $\square \div 6 = 6$

13. How many horseshoes are needed for 5 horses?

14. A class of 27 children get into groups of 3. How many groups are there?

15. How many sides do 3 hexagons have?

16. Four children can sit at one table. How many tables are needed for a class of 32?

C

Work out

1. 60×3
2. 30×3
3. 8×30
4. 5×30

5. 20×4
6. 90×4
7. 3×40
8. 7×40

9. 50×6
10. 80×6
11. 4×60
12. 7×60

13. $120 \div 3$
14. $270 \div 3$
15. $60 \div 3$
16. $210 \div 3$

17. $200 \div 4$
18. $320 \div 4$
19. $240 \div 4$
20. $160 \div 4$

21. $120 \div 6$
22. $360 \div 6$
23. $180 \div 6$
24. $540 \div 6$

25. There are 6 chairs in one stack. How many are there in 20 stacks?

26. Three packets of sweets weigh 240 g. What does one packet weigh?

27. One ice cream costs 70p. How much do four ice creams cost?

28. One box holds six eggs. How many boxes are needed for 480 eggs?

I can recognise when a word problem involves multiplication or division.

Before solving, sort the problems into two groups:
● problems involving multiplication
● problems involving division.

A

1. What is 6 times 2?
2. How many fives make 20?
3. Find 4 multiplied by 10.
4. Share 12 by 4.
5. What is 7 groups of 5?
6. Eight children wear boots. How many boots are there?
7. A starfish has 5 arms. How many arms do 5 starfish have?

8. Divide 100 by 10.
9. There are 30 children in a class. Half the children walk to school. How many children do not walk to school?
10. Each bag holds 10 sweets. How many sweets are there in 6 bags?

B

1. What is 36 divided by 6?
2. Find 3 lots of 40.
3. What is the product of 7 and 3?
4. How many teams of 4 can be made from 32 children?
5. Jack has 90 cm of string. He cuts it into 3 equal lengths. How long is each length?
6. What number is 9 times greater than 4?
7. Five people win a competition. They share the £1000 prize. How much should each person get?
8. Rose has 6 pens. Sharon has three times as many. How many pens does Sharon have?
9. There are 12 cubes in a block. There are 3 blocks. How many cubes are there?
10. There are 24 children in a class. One in every four has green eyes. How many children have green eyes?

C

1. A pack of eight cans of drink costs £6·00. How much does each can cost?
2. Find the product of the smallest 2-digit number and the largest 2-digit number.
3. There are 48 passengers on a bus. One in every three is a man. How many men are on the bus?
4. Which number, when divided by 15, gives an answer of 5?
5. One fifth of the paper clips in a packet are yellow. There are 20 yellow paper clips. How many paper clips are there in the packet?
6. A tray of plants holds six flowers. How many trays can be filled from 54 flowers?

I can find a multiplication calculation linked to a division calculation, or vice versa.

Knowing one × or ÷ fact means that you know three related facts.

Examples

6 × 3 = 18   3 × 6 = 18   4 × ☐ = 28
18 ÷ 6 = 3   18 ÷ 3 = 6   The answer is 7 because 28 ÷ 4 = 7

A

Copy and complete these related facts.

1 5 × 4 = 20
   4 × ☐ = 20
   20 ÷ ☐ = 5
   20 ÷ ☐ = 4

2 8 × 2 = ☐
   ☐ × 8 = 16
   16 ÷ ☐ = 8
   16 ÷ ☐ = ☐

Copy and complete.

3 7 × ☐ = 14

4 8 × ☐ = 40

5 ☐ × 10 = 70

6 ☐ × 2 = 18

7 35 ÷ ☐ = 7

8 100 ÷ ☐ = 10

9 ☐ ÷ 2 = 12

10 ☐ ÷ 5 = 3

11 I think of a number. I multiply by 10. The answer is 80. What was my number?

B

Write three linked × or ÷ facts for each fact given.

1 2 × 10 = 20

2 12 × 5 = 60

3 27 ÷ 3 = 9

4 88 ÷ 11 = 8

Copy and complete.

5 ☐ × 6 = 54

6 ☐ ÷ 3 = 10

7 8 × ☐ = 32

8 45 ÷ ☐ = 9

9 Multiply 6 by 2. Divide your answer by 2. What do you notice?

10 Divide 40 by 5. Multiply your answer by 5. What do you notice?

11 I think of a number. I multiply by 4 and then subtract 3. The answer is 25. What was my number?

12 I think of a number. I divide by 6 and add 2. The answer is 12. What was my number?

C

Write four different × or ÷ facts for each group of numbers.

1 42   6   7

2 5   20   100

3 8   72   9

4 90   15   6

5 What number, when multiplied by 3 and then divided by 6, gives an answer of 4?

6 What number, when divided by 4 and then multiplied by 5, gives an answer of 30?

Copy and complete the multiplication squares.

7

×		7	
			24
	45	63	
8			48

8

×	8		
		63	21
10			30
		54	

I can use doubling or halving to find new facts using known facts.

Examples

Double and double
to multiply by 4
$12 \times 4 = 48$ (12, 24, 48)
$30 \times 4 = 120$ (30, 60, 120)

Using doubling to calculate.
Find 9×8
$9 \times 4 = 36$
$9 \times 8 = 72$ (36×2)

Find 5×14
$5 \times 7 = 35$
$5 \times 14 = 70$ (35×2)

Halve and halve
again to find
one quarter.
Find $\frac{1}{4}$ of 60
$\frac{1}{2}$ of $60 = 30$
$\frac{1}{4}$ of $60 = 15$

A

Double and double again to multiply each number by 4.

1. 7
2. 5
3. 6
4. 10
5. 20
6. 3
7. 4
8. 9
9. 8
10. 100

Double the first answer to work out the second.

11. 2×4
    2×8
12. 7×3
    7×6
13. 2×6
    2×12
14. 10×4
    20×4
15. 7×2
    14×2
16. 4×3
    8×3

Use squared paper. Draw each shape half the size of the measurements shown.

17. [rectangle] 20 cm, 8 cm

18. [square] 6 cm, 6 cm, 12 cm, 12 cm

B

Double and double again to multiply each number by 4.

1. 13
2. 11
3. 17
4. 16
5. 30
6. 15
7. 25
8. 35
9. 45
10. 50

Double the first answer to work out the second.

11. 40×3
    40×6
12. 8×4
    8×8
13. 5×6
    5×12
14. 10×30
    20×30
15. 6×3
    12×3
16. 8×5
    16×5

17. Use squared paper. Draw the flag half the size of the measurements shown.

[flag] 20 cm, 24 cm, 20 cm, 40 cm

18. Now draw the flag one quarter the size of the measurements shown.

C

Double and double again to multiply each number by 4.

1. 29
2. 42
3. 27
4. 31
5. 120
6. 22
7. 36
8. 55
9. 75
10. 250

Double the first answer to work out the second.

11. 14×3
    14×6
12. 25×4
    25×8
13. 23×10
    23×20
14. 6×7
    12×7
15. 4×12
    8×12
16. 2×15
    4×15

17. Use squared paper. Draw the flag one quarter the size of the measurements shown.

[flag] 20 cm, 20 cm, 12 cm, 12 cm, 48 cm

18. Now draw the flag one eighth size.

I can multiply one and two-digit numbers by 10 and 100 and one-digit numbers by multiples of 10.

Examples

$6 \times 10 = 60$

$62 \times 10 = 620$

$3 \times 100 = 300$

$35 \times 100 = 3500$

$70 \div 10 = 7$

$740 \div 10 = 74$

$5 \times 30 = 5 \times 3 \times 10$

$\quad = 15 \times 10$

$\quad = 150$

A

Work out

1 5×10 9 13×10

2 2×10 10 58×10

3 4×10 11 24×10

4 9×10 12 71×10

5 6×10 13 39×10

6 8×10 14 62×10

7 3×10 15 97×10

8 7×10 16 46×10

Copy and complete.

17 $3 \times 20 = 3 \times \square \times 10$

$\quad = \square \times 10$

$\quad = \square$

18 $6 \times 50 = 6 \times \square \times \square$

$\quad = \square \times \square$

$\quad = \square$

19 $7 \times 30 = 7 \times \square \times 10$

$\quad = \square \times 10$

$\quad = \square$

20 $5 \times 40 = \square \times 4 \times \square$

$\quad = \square \times \square$

$\quad = \square$

B

Copy and complete.

1 $\square \times 10 = 310$

2 $\square \times 10 = 460$

3 $\square \times 10 = 170$

4 $\square \times 10 = 820$

5 $\square \div 10 = 25$

6 $\square \div 10 = 83$

7 $\square \div 10 = 59$

8 $\square \div 10 = 74$

9 $2 \times 100 = \square$

10 $10 \times 100 = \square$

11 $\square \times 100 = 900$

12 $\square \times 100 = 500$

Work out

13 4×20 17 4×60

14 3×40 18 9×20

15 6×30 19 7×50

16 5×50 20 2×80

Copy and complete.

21 $240 \div 40 = \square$

22 $300 \div 6 = \square$

23 $270 \div \square = 3$

24 $400 \div \square = 50$

C

Copy and complete.

1 $46 \times 10 = \square$

2 $8 \times 100 = \square$

3 $67 \times \square = 6700$

4 $135 \times \square = 1350$

5 $\square \times 10 = 400$

6 $\square \times 100 = 700$

7 $240 \div 10 = \square$

8 $5800 \div 100 = \square$

9 $190 \div \square = 19$

10 $4400 \div \square = 44$

11 $\square \div 100 = 30$

12 $\square \div 10 = 280$

Work out

13 7×60 17 9×500

14 3×90 18 5×800

15 8×40 19 4×700

16 6×60 20 3×600

Copy and complete.

21 $540 \div 90 = \square$

22 $480 \div 6 = \square$

23 $2400 \div 300 = \square$

24 $4500 \div 5 = \square$

I can work out remainders when dividing.

Example
13 marbles are shared equally between 3 children.

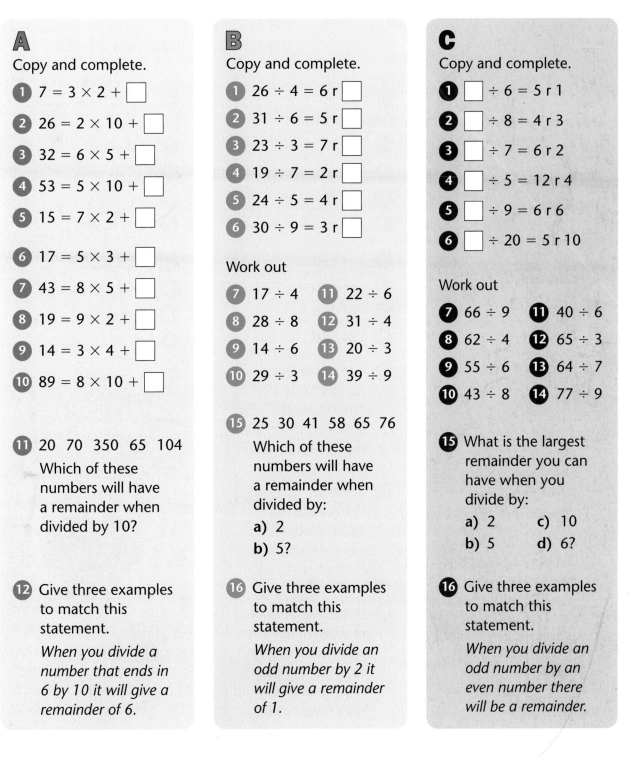

Each child gets 4 marbles and there is one marble left over.

$13 \div 3 = 4 \, r \, 1$ (4 remainder 1)

A

Copy and complete.

1. $7 = 3 \times 2 + \square$
2. $26 = 2 \times 10 + \square$
3. $32 = 6 \times 5 + \square$
4. $53 = 5 \times 10 + \square$
5. $15 = 7 \times 2 + \square$
6. $17 = 5 \times 3 + \square$
7. $43 = 8 \times 5 + \square$
8. $19 = 9 \times 2 + \square$
9. $14 = 3 \times 4 + \square$
10. $89 = 8 \times 10 + \square$

11. 20 70 350 65 104

Which of these numbers will have a remainder when divided by 10?

12. Give three examples to match this statement.

When you divide a number that ends in 6 by 10 it will give a remainder of 6.

B

Copy and complete.

1. $26 \div 4 = 6 \, r \, \square$
2. $31 \div 6 = 5 \, r \, \square$
3. $23 \div 3 = 7 \, r \, \square$
4. $19 \div 7 = 2 \, r \, \square$
5. $24 \div 5 = 4 \, r \, \square$
6. $30 \div 9 = 3 \, r \, \square$

Work out

7. $17 \div 4$
8. $28 \div 8$
9. $14 \div 6$
10. $29 \div 3$
11. $22 \div 6$
12. $31 \div 4$
13. $20 \div 3$
14. $39 \div 9$

15. 25 30 41 58 65 76

Which of these numbers will have a remainder when divided by:
a) 2
b) 5?

16. Give three examples to match this statement.

When you divide an odd number by 2 it will give a remainder of 1.

C

Copy and complete.

1. $\square \div 6 = 5 \, r \, 1$
2. $\square \div 8 = 4 \, r \, 3$
3. $\square \div 7 = 6 \, r \, 2$
4. $\square \div 5 = 12 \, r \, 4$
5. $\square \div 9 = 6 \, r \, 6$
6. $\square \div 20 = 5 \, r \, 10$

Work out

7. $66 \div 9$
8. $62 \div 4$
9. $55 \div 6$
10. $43 \div 8$
11. $40 \div 6$
12. $65 \div 3$
13. $64 \div 7$
14. $77 \div 9$

15. What is the largest remainder you can have when you divide by:
a) 2   c) 10
b) 5   d) 6?

16. Give three examples to match this statement.

When you divide an odd number by an even number there will be a remainder.

I can solve word problems involving division and find fractions of sets of objects.

Examples

Twelve sweets are shared equally between 6 children.
How many do they have each?
$12 \div 6 = 2$
They have 2 sweets each.

Find one third of 12 counters.

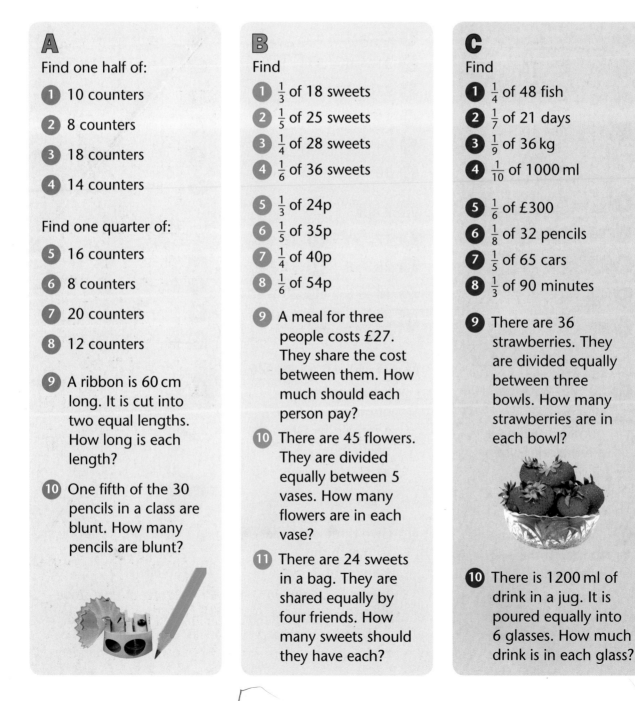

$\frac{1}{3}$ of $12 = 12 \div 3 = 4$
One third of 12 counters is 4 counters.

A

Find one half of:

1. 10 counters
2. 8 counters
3. 18 counters
4. 14 counters

Find one quarter of:

5. 16 counters
6. 8 counters
7. 20 counters
8. 12 counters

9. A ribbon is 60 cm long. It is cut into two equal lengths. How long is each length?

10. One fifth of the 30 pencils in a class are blunt. How many pencils are blunt?

B

Find

1. $\frac{1}{3}$ of 18 sweets
2. $\frac{1}{5}$ of 25 sweets
3. $\frac{1}{4}$ of 28 sweets
4. $\frac{1}{6}$ of 36 sweets

5. $\frac{1}{3}$ of 24p
6. $\frac{1}{5}$ of 35p
7. $\frac{1}{4}$ of 40p
8. $\frac{1}{6}$ of 54p

9. A meal for three people costs £27. They share the cost between them. How much should each person pay?

10. There are 45 flowers. They are divided equally between 5 vases. How many flowers are in each vase?

11. There are 24 sweets in a bag. They are shared equally by four friends. How many sweets should they have each?

C

Find

1. $\frac{1}{4}$ of 48 fish
2. $\frac{1}{7}$ of 21 days
3. $\frac{1}{9}$ of 36 kg
4. $\frac{1}{10}$ of 1000 ml

5. $\frac{1}{6}$ of £300
6. $\frac{1}{8}$ of 32 pencils
7. $\frac{1}{5}$ of 65 cars
8. $\frac{1}{3}$ of 90 minutes

9. There are 36 strawberries. They are divided equally between three bowls. How many strawberries are in each bowl?

10. There is 1200 ml of drink in a jug. It is poured equally into 6 glasses. How much drink is in each glass?

I can read, write and understand fractions and I can compare them.

Examples

2 equal parts

$\frac{1}{2}$

one half is shaded

5 equal parts

$\frac{1}{5}$

one fifth is shaded

3 equal parts

$\frac{1}{3}$

one third is shaded

A

What fraction of each shape is shaded?

1 5

2 6

3 7

4 8

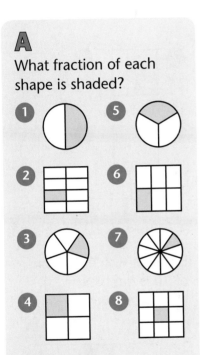

Complete these sentences by writing the fraction in words.

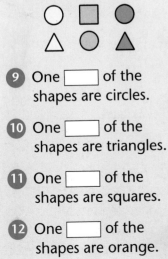

9 One ☐ of the shapes are circles.

10 One ☐ of the shapes are triangles.

11 One ☐ of the shapes are squares.

12 One ☐ of the shapes are orange.

B

What fraction is shown on each number line?

1 0 ─────↓────── 1

2 0 ─↓──────── 1

3 0 ↓───────── 1

4 0 ───↓────── 1

5 Find the six different ways of shading one half of this square.

Use five strips of 12 squares.

6 Shade $\frac{1}{2}$ of strip 1.

Shade $\frac{1}{3}$ of strip 2.

Shade $\frac{1}{4}$ of strip 3.

Shade $\frac{1}{6}$ of strip 4

Shade $\frac{1}{12}$ of strip 5.

Look at your strips. Which fraction is:
a) largest
b) smallest?

C

Write these fractions in order, smallest first.

1 $\frac{1}{2}$ $\frac{1}{5}$ $\frac{1}{4}$

2 $\frac{1}{7}$ $\frac{1}{10}$ $\frac{1}{3}$

3 $\frac{1}{2}$ $\frac{1}{9}$ $\frac{1}{100}$

4 $\frac{1}{8}$ $\frac{1}{3}$ $\frac{1}{12}$

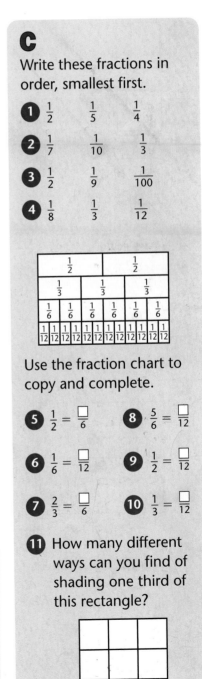

Use the fraction chart to copy and complete.

5 $\frac{1}{2} = \frac{\square}{6}$ 8 $\frac{5}{6} = \frac{\square}{12}$

6 $\frac{1}{6} = \frac{\square}{12}$ 9 $\frac{1}{2} = \frac{\square}{12}$

7 $\frac{2}{3} = \frac{\square}{6}$ 10 $\frac{1}{3} = \frac{\square}{12}$

11 How many different ways can you find of shading one third of this rectangle?

I can estimate a fraction of a shape and the number an arrow is pointing to on a number line.

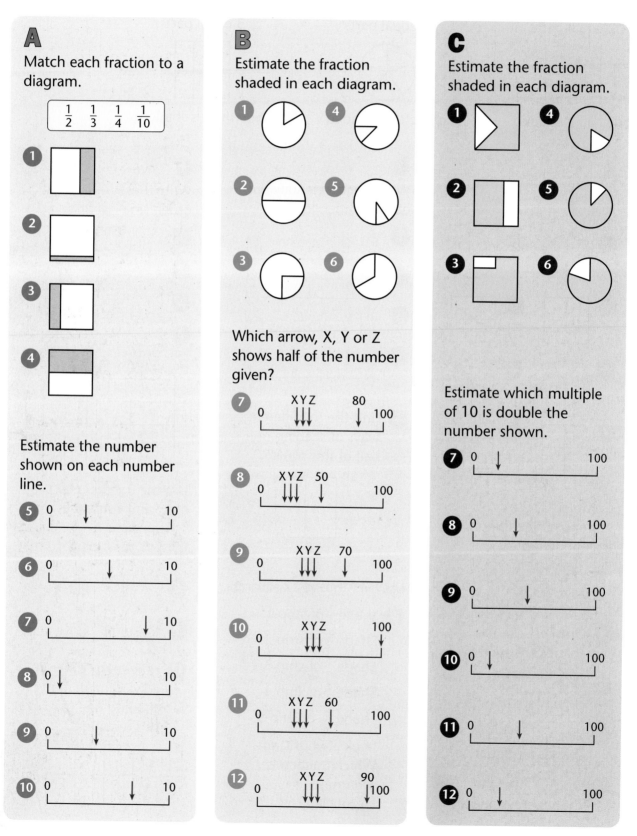

A
Match each fraction to a diagram.

$$\frac{1}{2} \quad \frac{1}{3} \quad \frac{1}{4} \quad \frac{1}{10}$$

1

2

3

4

Estimate the number shown on each number line.

5 0 ↓ 10

6 0 ↓ 10

7 0 ↓ 10

8 0 ↓ 10

9 0 ↓ 10

10 0 ↓ 10

B
Estimate the fraction shaded in each diagram.

1   **4**

2   **5**

3   **6**

Which arrow, X, Y or Z shows half of the number given?

7   X Y Z   80
     0 ↓↓↓   ↓ 100

8   X Y Z 50
     0 ↓↓↓ ↓   100

9   X Y Z   70
     0 ↓↓↓   ↓ 100

10   X Y Z   100
     0   ↓↓↓   ↓

11   X Y Z   60
     0 ↓↓↓   ↓ 100

12   X Y Z   90
     0 ↓↓↓   ↓ 100

C
Estimate the fraction shaded in each diagram.

1   **4**

2   **5**

3   **6**

Estimate which multiple of 10 is double the number shown.

7 0 ↓   100

8 0   ↓ 100

9 0   ↓ 100

10 0 ↓   100

11 0   ↓ 100

12 0   ↓ 100

I can count on and back and recognise when the numbers in a counting sequence are odd or even.

Examples
- count on in 2s from 3   3 5 7 9 11 13   odd numbers only
- count on in 3s from 2   2 5 8 11 14 17   even, odd, even, odd
- count on in 2s from 10   10 12 14 16 18 20   even numbers only
- count on in 3s from 1   1 4 7 10 13 16   odd, even, odd, even

A

Write the first six numbers in each sequence.

1. Start from 5. Count on in 2s.

2. Start from 91. Count on in 10s.

3. Start from 7. Count on in 5s.

4. Start from 29. Count on in 4s.

5. Start from 15. Count on in 3s.

6. Start from 24. Count on in 2s.

What is the pattern of odd and even numbers in each sequence.

7. 3 5 7 9

8. 4 7 10 13

9. 4 8 12 16

10. 5 10 15 20

11. 2 4 6 8

12. 3 6 9 12

B

Write the next three numbers in each sequence.

1. 57 54 51 48

2. 38 42 46 50

3. 76 78 80 82

4. 63 68 73 78

5. 84 78 72 66

6. 10 30 50 70

What is the pattern of odd and even numbers if you:

7. count on in 2s from 5

8. count on in 5s from 2

9. count on in 6s from 10

10. count on in 10s from 6

11. count on in 3s from 4

12. count on in 4s from 3

Copy and continue each sequence to 100.

13. 1, 11, 12, 22, 23, 33...

14. 4, 14, 16, 26, 28, 38...

15. 3 $_{21}$ 24 $_{21}$ 45 $_{21}$...

16. 1 $_{15}$ 16 $_{15}$ 31 $_{15}$...

C

Copy each sequence and write the next three numbers.

1. 66 59 52 45

2. 13 24 35 46

3. 90 98 106 114

4. 150 135 120 105

5. 4 13 22 31

6. 75 100 125 150

7. What number did I start from if I count on six steps of 7 and reach 45?

8. What number did I start from if I count back four steps of 15 and I am left with 74?

9. Write a sequence of six steps counting back in 8s where all the numbers are even.

10. Write a sequence of six steps counting back in 6s where all the numbers are odd.

I can find the relevant information to solve word problems.

Example
There are 8 camels. They travel 12 km. There are two people on each camel. How many people are travelling in the camel train?

$8 \times 2 = 16$
Answer *16 people*
They travel 12 km is not relevant information.

A

1. There are 30 children in a class. Sixteen are boys. Twelve children have brown hair. How many girls are in the class?

2. Martin has two piles of 6 books and three piles of 5 books. How many books does he have altogether?

3. Helen is 33 years old. Sally is 20 years older than Helen. Gill is 48. How old is Sally?

4. There are 20 motorcycles in a shop. One half are red. One quarter are blue. How many red motorcycles are there?

5. Ben has a piece of wood one metre long. He saws off 50 cm. He saws off another 20 cm. How much wood is left?

B

1. Megan buys two comics for 35p each. She pays £1. How much change does she have?

2. Large cans of fish weigh 400 g. Small cans weigh half as much. What do four small cans weigh?

3. A bottle of drink costs 60p. It holds 900 ml. It is shared by three children. How much drink do they each have?

4. There are 70 apples on a tree. 25 apples are picked. Eight more fall off. How many apples are left on the tree?

5. The top shelf of a bookcase has 45 books. The middle shelf has 52 books. The bottom shelf has 23 more books than the top shelf. How many books are on the bottom shelf?

6. There are 48 biscuits in a tin. Half of them are eaten. 13 more are eaten. How many biscuits are left?

C

1. There are 84 cars parked in a car park. 67 more cars are parked. 54 cars drive out. How many cars are left in the car park?

2. In one week a cyclist rides 15 km on four days and 25 km on three days. How far does she cycle in the week altogether?

3. Ethan takes four minutes to read one page. He is on page 73. How many pages does he read in one hour?

4. A jar holds two litres of juice. This is poured equally into 10 glasses. How much does each glass hold?

5. Esther has £2. She spends 75p and 47p. How much does she have left?

6. There are 65 adults and 47 children on a train. Tickets cost £5. How many people are there on the train?

I can use partitioning to add and subtract numbers.

Examples   68 + 45

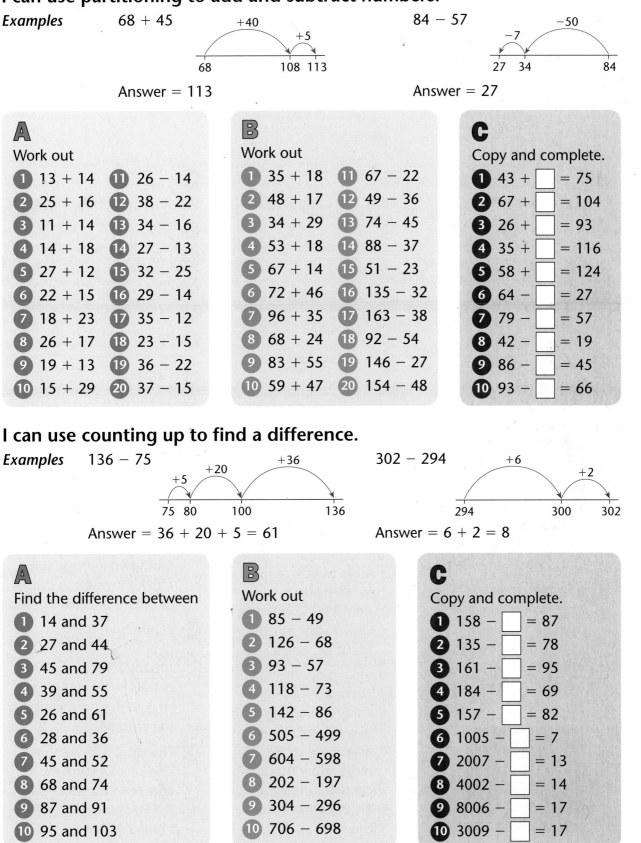

Answer = 113

84 − 57

Answer = 27

A

Work out

1. 13 + 14   11. 26 − 14
2. 25 + 16   12. 38 − 22
3. 11 + 14   13. 34 − 16
4. 14 + 18   14. 27 − 13
5. 27 + 12   15. 32 − 25
6. 22 + 15   16. 29 − 14
7. 18 + 23   17. 35 − 12
8. 26 + 17   18. 23 − 15
9. 19 + 13   19. 36 − 22
10. 15 + 29   20. 37 − 15

B

Work out

1. 35 + 18   11. 67 − 22
2. 48 + 17   12. 49 − 36
3. 34 + 29   13. 74 − 45
4. 53 + 18   14. 88 − 37
5. 67 + 14   15. 51 − 23
6. 72 + 46   16. 135 − 32
7. 96 + 35   17. 163 − 38
8. 68 + 24   18. 92 − 54
9. 83 + 55   19. 146 − 27
10. 59 + 47   20. 154 − 48

C

Copy and complete.

1. 43 + ☐ = 75
2. 67 + ☐ = 104
3. 26 + ☐ = 93
4. 35 + ☐ = 116
5. 58 + ☐ = 124
6. 64 − ☐ = 27
7. 79 − ☐ = 57
8. 42 − ☐ = 19
9. 86 − ☐ = 45
10. 93 − ☐ = 66

I can use counting up to find a difference.

Examples   136 − 75

Answer = 36 + 20 + 5 = 61

302 − 294

Answer = 6 + 2 = 8

A

Find the difference between

1. 14 and 37
2. 27 and 44
3. 45 and 79
4. 39 and 55
5. 26 and 61
6. 28 and 36
7. 45 and 52
8. 68 and 74
9. 87 and 91
10. 95 and 103

B

Work out

1. 85 − 49
2. 126 − 68
3. 93 − 57
4. 118 − 73
5. 142 − 86
6. 505 − 499
7. 604 − 598
8. 202 − 197
9. 304 − 296
10. 706 − 698

C

Copy and complete.

1. 158 − ☐ = 87
2. 135 − ☐ = 78
3. 161 − ☐ = 95
4. 184 − ☐ = 69
5. 157 − ☐ = 82
6. 1005 − ☐ = 7
7. 2007 − ☐ = 13
8. 4002 − ☐ = 14
9. 8006 − ☐ = 17
10. 3009 − ☐ = 17

I can use a written method for addition calculations.

Examples

66 + 58

```
   66
 +  8
   74
 + 50
  124
```

$$66 = 60 + 6$$
$$+58 = 50 + 8$$
$$110 + 14 = 124$$

$$174 = 100 + 70 + 4$$
$$+156 = 100 + 50 + 6$$
$$200 + 120 + 10 = 330$$

A

Copy and complete.

1. 33
    +24

2. 42
    +25

3. 37
    +32

4. 51
    +28

5. 65
    +33

6. 38
    +26

7. 55
    +37

8. 49
    +45

9. 56
    +27

10. 58
    +39

11. A squirrel hides 47 nuts in one hole and 36 nuts in another hole. How many nuts does the squirrel have hidden away altogether?

B

Copy and complete.

1. 49
    +39

2. 66
    +45

3. 58
    +54

4. 89
    +35

5. 74
    +68

6. 97
    +84

7. 68
    +57

8. 93
    +38

9. 85
    +66

10. 79
    +54

11. Anita buys a pen for 89p and a pencil for 25p. How much has she spent altogether?

12. There are 76 children on the playground. They are joined by 58 more. How many children are there on the playground now?

C

Set out as in the example.

1. 164 + 147

2. 179 + 159

3. 286 + 128

4. 348 + 275

5. 297 + 136

6. 156 + 144

7. 372 + 269

8. 465 + 286

9. 238 + 148

10. 529 + 377

11. Garry bought a washing machine for £369 and a fridge for £254. How much did he spend altogether?

12. In one hour 435 people went into the supermarket and 387 people left. How many people passed through the entrance?

13. There are 118 cars on Level 1 of a car park and 164 cars on Level 2. How many cars are in the car park?

I can use a written method for subtraction calculations.

Examples

94 − 36

94 = 90 + 4 = 80 + 14
−36 = 30 + 6 = 30 + 6
_____
            50 + 8 = 58

232 − 46

232 = 200 + 30 + 2 = 100 + 120 + 12
 − 46 = _____ 40 + 6 = _____ 40 + 6
_____
                    100 + 80 + 6 = 186

A

Copy and complete.

1. 37
   −18

2. 53
   −35

3. 68
   −42

4. 82
   −46

5. 73
   −56

6. 91
   −37

7. 46
   −29

8. 77
   −32

9. 53
   −28

10. 64
    −25

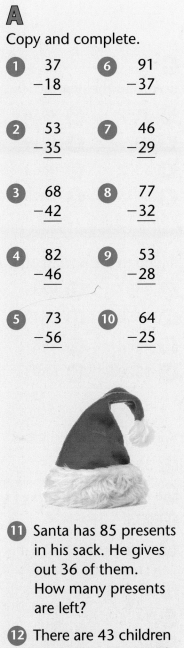

11. Santa has 85 presents in his sack. He gives out 36 of them. How many presents are left?

12. There are 43 children at a party. 26 are girls. How many are boys?

B

Copy and complete.

1. 64
   − 37

2. 94
   − 48

3. 181
   − 57

4. 136
   − 83

5. 243
   − 71

6. 125
   − 49

7. 158
   − 64

8. 132
   − 77

9. 154
   − 86

10. 163
    − 75

11. A baker makes 117 cakes. 79 are sold. How many cakes are left?

12. There are 225 birds on a telephone wire. 93 fly off. How many birds are left?

13. A new bicycle costs £149. Serena has £85. How much more does she need?

C

Set out as in the examples.

1. 245 − 138

2. 367 − 183

3. 541 − 425

4. 769 − 383

5. 854 − 289

6. 935 − 472

7. 621 − 367

8. 418 − 182

9. 630 − 297

10. 506 − 355

11. There are 347 people in a cinema. 209 of them are children. How many are adults?

12. A television normally costs £729. In a sale Tara paid £584. How much did she save?

13. Roy has a journey of 412 miles. He drives 136 miles. How much further does he have to go?

I can round numbers to the nearest 10 or 100 and use rounding to estimate a sum or difference.

TO NEAREST 10
Look at the units.
5 or more, round up.
Below 5, round down.

Examples
39 rounds to 40
34 rounds to 30

TO NEAREST 100
Look at 10s and units.
50 or more, round up.
Below 50, round down.

Examples
450 rounds to 500
448 rounds to 400

APPROXIMATING
$326 + 53 \rightarrow 330 + 50 \rightarrow 380$
$219 - 72 \rightarrow 220 - 70 \rightarrow 150$
$62 \times 3 \rightarrow 60 \times 3 \rightarrow 180$

A

Copy and complete.

1. 46 rounds to ☐
2. 83 rounds to ☐
3. 31 rounds to ☐
4. 29 rounds to ☐

Round to the nearest 10.

5. 17
6. 65
7. 94
8. 27
9. 43
10. 52
11. 38
12. 75

Approximate by rounding.

13. 36 + 22
14. 53 + 37
15. 25 + 64
16. 41 + 58

17. 72 − 23
18. 96 − 78
19. 89 − 52
20. 61 − 49

B

Round to the nearest 10.

1. 62
2. 74
3. 26
4. 93
5. 59
6. 135
7. 187
8. 18

Round to the nearest 100.

9. 210
10. 560
11. 157
12. 784
13. 472
14. 661
15. 329
16. 815

Approximate by rounding.

17. 62 + 33
18. 139 + 14
19. 43 + 26
20. 57 + 99

21. 92 − 51
22. 129 − 67
23. 71 − 48
24. 119 − 82

C

Round to the nearest 10.

1. 3152
2. 737
3. 6372
4. 5145
5. 4956
6. 1219
7. 9663
8. 7095

Round to the nearest 100.

9. 3487
10. 1650
11. 8832
12. 5370
13. 9725
14. 2649
15. 4981
16. 6893

Approximate by rounding.

17. 398 + 57
18. 169 + 41
19. 235 − 194
20. 376 − 138

21. 47 × 3
22. 54 × 5
23. 86 × 4
24. 23 × 6

I can work systematically to solve problems.

Examples

A shop sells bicycles and tricycles.
Each morning Carl pumps up all the tyres.
Today he pumps up 19 tyres.
How many bicycles are in the shop and how
many tricycles? Find all the solutions.

METHOD
Write out the 2 times table and the 3 times table.
Take one number from each list to make 19.

SOLUTIONS
The shop has:

        2 bicycles and 5 tricycles

or   *5 bicycles and 3 tricycles*

or   *8 bicycles and 1 tricycle.*

$1 \times 2 = 2$	$1 \times 3 = 3$
$2 \times 2 = 4$	$2 \times 3 = 6$
$3 \times 2 = 6$	$3 \times 3 = 9$
$4 \times 2 = 8$	$4 \times 3 = 12$
$5 \times 2 = 10$	$5 \times 3 = 15$
$6 \times 2 = 12$	$6 \times 3 = 18$
$7 \times 2 = 14$	
$8 \times 2 = 16$	
$9 \times 2 = 18$	
$10 \times 2 = 20$	

A

THE PROBLEM
Jasmin has 5ps and 10ps
only. Altogether she has
45p.
How many 5ps does she
have and how many
10ps? Find all the possible
solutions.

METHOD

1. Write out the 5 times
   table to 45.

2. Write out the 10
   times table to 40.

3. Take one number
   from each list to
   make 45.

4. Find the five possible
   solutions.

B

THE PROBLEM
There are 26 children
in a class. Some of the
children sit in pairs. The
rest of the class sit at
tables of 4.
How many children sit in
pairs and how many at
tables of 4?

METHOD

1. Write out the 2 times
   table to 24.

2. Write out the 4 times
   table to 24.

3. Take one number
   from each list to
   make 26.

4. Find the six possible
   solutions.

C

1. Nita has 22 straws.
   She uses them all to
   make triangles and
   squares. How many
   triangles does she
   make and how many
   squares? Find all the
   possible solutions.

2. Christmas balls are
   sold in packets of 3
   or packets of 5. Jamie
   buys 29 balls. How
   many packets of 3
   does he buy and how
   many packets of 5?
   Find all the possible
   solutions.

I can multiply and divide multiples of 10.

Examples

$50 \times 3 = 10 \times 5 \times 3$ $80 \times 2 = 10 \times 8 \times 2$ $90 \div 3 = 10 \times 9 \div 3$ $80 \div 4 = 10 \times 8 \div 4$
$\qquad\quad = 10 \times 15$ $\qquad\quad = 10 \times 16$ $\qquad\quad = 10 \times 3$ $\qquad\quad = 10 \times 2$
$\qquad\quad = 150$ $\qquad\quad = 160$ $\qquad\quad = 30$ $\qquad\quad = 20$

A

Multiply by 10.

1. 4
2. 2
3. 9
4. 16
5. 25
6. 8
7. 13
8. 75

Divide by 10.

9. 50
10. 120
11. 70
12. 60
13. 100
14. 30
15. 480
16. 210

Copy and complete.

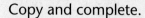

17. $60 \times 2 = 10 \times \boxed{} \times 2$
    $\qquad = 10 \times \boxed{}$
    $\qquad = \boxed{}$

18. $30 \times 4 = 10 \times \boxed{} \times 4$
    $\qquad = 10 \times \boxed{}$
    $\qquad = \boxed{}$

19. $150 \div 3 = 10 \times \boxed{} \div 3$
    $\qquad = 10 \times \boxed{}$
    $\qquad = \boxed{}$

20. $300 \div 5 = 10 \times \boxed{} \div 5$
    $\qquad = 10 \times \boxed{}$
    $\qquad = \boxed{}$

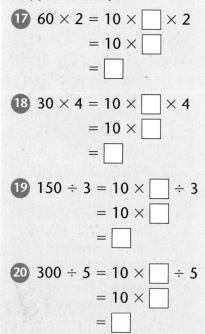

B

Work out

1. 20×3
2. 50×5
3. 90×2
4. 20×4
5. 50×6
6. 70×3
7. 60×4
8. 30×6
9. $320 \div 4$
10. $80 \div 2$
11. $120 \div 6$
12. $400 \div 5$
13. $270 \div 3$
14. $140 \div 2$
15. $150 \div 5$
16. $240 \div 6$

17. One lolly costs 70p. What do four lollies cost?

18. A car travels at a speed of 60 miles every hour. How far will it travel in 5 hours?

19. There are 120 pins in two packets. The packets are the same. How many pins are there in each packet?

20. Three packets of crisps weigh 120 g. What does one packet weigh?

C

Work out

1. 70×6
2. 40×8
3. 50×7
4. 90×4
5. 20×8
6. 30×6
7. 80×9
8. 90×5
9. $240 \div 3$
10. $280 \div 7$
11. $360 \div 6$
12. $480 \div 8$
13. $630 \div 9$
14. $560 \div 7$
15. $240 \div 8$
16. $540 \div 6$

17. There are 30 children in each class. There are seven classes in the school. How many children are there in the school?

18. One card costs 40p. What do nine cards cost?

19. Daisy walks 480 metres in six minutes. How far does she walk in one minute?

20. Eight eggs weigh 560 g. What does one egg weigh?

I can multiply or divide a two-digit number by partitioning.

Examples

56 × 3 = 50 × 3 plus 6 × 3
= 150 plus 18
= 168

84 ÷ 2 = 80 ÷ 2 plus 4 ÷ 2
= 40 plus 2
= 42

A

Copy and complete.

1 14 × 2
= 10 × 2 plus 4 × 2
= ☐ plus ☐
= ☐

2 21 × 4
= 20 × 4 plus 1 × 4
= ☐ plus ☐
= ☐

3 33 × 3
= 30 × 3 plus 3 × 3
= ☐ plus ☐
= ☐

4 64 ÷ 2
= 60 ÷ 2 plus 4 ÷ 2
= ☐ plus ☐
= ☐

5 93 ÷ 3
= 90 ÷ 3 plus 3 ÷ 3
= ☐ plus ☐
= ☐

6 48 ÷ 4
= 40 ÷ 4 plus 8 ÷ 4
= ☐ plus ☐
= ☐

B

Work out

1 38 × 3 **9** 82 ÷ 2
2 25 × 4 **10** 63 ÷ 3
3 43 × 2 **11** 88 ÷ 4
4 27 × 5 **12** 55 ÷ 5
5 14 × 6 **13** 64 ÷ 2
6 45 × 3 **14** 96 ÷ 3
7 36 × 4 **15** 44 ÷ 4
8 57 × 2 **16** 39 ÷ 3

17 Use each of the digits 2, 3 and 4 once only. Complete this calculation in six different ways.

☐☐ × ☐

Which calculation gives:
a) the largest product
b) the smallest product?

18 Use three of the digits 3, 4, 5 and 6 to complete this calculation in different ways:

☐☐ × ☐

Which calculation gives:
a) the largest product
b) the smallest product?

C

Work out

1 59 × 3 **9** 126 ÷ 2
2 74 × 4 **10** 156 ÷ 3
3 86 × 5 **11** 168 ÷ 4
4 32 × 6 **12** 155 ÷ 5
5 17 × 7 **13** 248 ÷ 2
6 25 × 8 **14** 219 ÷ 3
7 34 × 9 **15** 204 ÷ 4
8 56 × 6 **16** 126 ÷ 6

17 There are eight apples in each bag. How many bags are needed for 328 apples?

18 One coach can carry 65 passengers. How many passengers can seven coaches carry?

19 One rotation of the London Eye takes 32 minutes. How long will four rotations take?

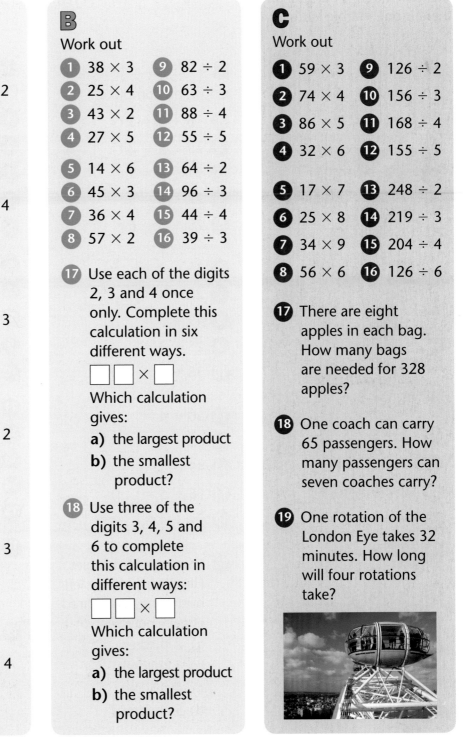

I can divide two-digit numbers by one-digit numbers and work out remainders.

Example

13 marbles are shared equally between 3 children.

Each child gets 4 marbles and there is one marble left over.

13 ÷ 3 = 4 r 1 (4 remainder 1)

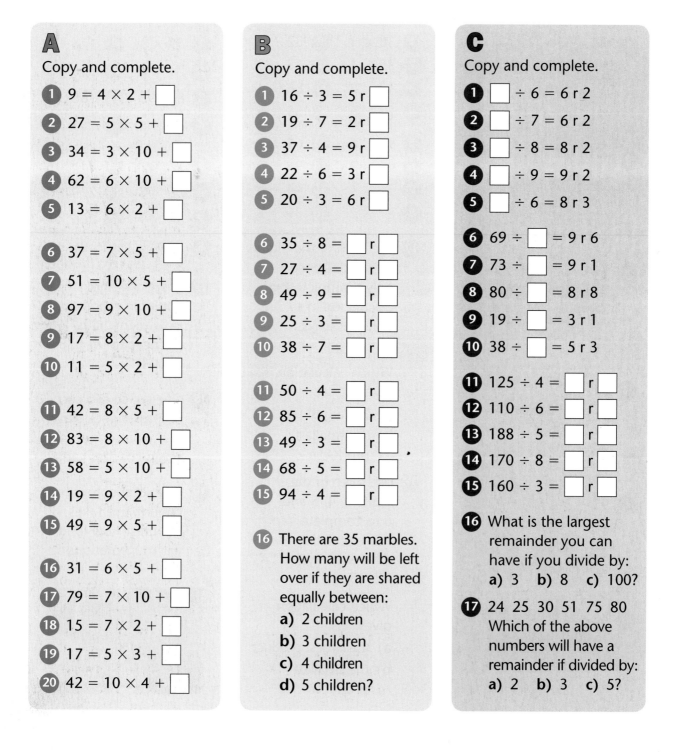

A

Copy and complete.

1. 9 = 4 × 2 + ☐
2. 27 = 5 × 5 + ☐
3. 34 = 3 × 10 + ☐
4. 62 = 6 × 10 + ☐
5. 13 = 6 × 2 + ☐

6. 37 = 7 × 5 + ☐
7. 51 = 10 × 5 + ☐
8. 97 = 9 × 10 + ☐
9. 17 = 8 × 2 + ☐
10. 11 = 5 × 2 + ☐

11. 42 = 8 × 5 + ☐
12. 83 = 8 × 10 + ☐
13. 58 = 5 × 10 + ☐
14. 19 = 9 × 2 + ☐
15. 49 = 9 × 5 + ☐

16. 31 = 6 × 5 + ☐
17. 79 = 7 × 10 + ☐
18. 15 = 7 × 2 + ☐
19. 17 = 5 × 3 + ☐
20. 42 = 10 × 4 + ☐

B

Copy and complete.

1. 16 ÷ 3 = 5 r ☐
2. 19 ÷ 7 = 2 r ☐
3. 37 ÷ 4 = 9 r ☐
4. 22 ÷ 6 = 3 r ☐
5. 20 ÷ 3 = 6 r ☐

6. 35 ÷ 8 = ☐ r ☐
7. 27 ÷ 4 = ☐ r ☐
8. 49 ÷ 9 = ☐ r ☐
9. 25 ÷ 3 = ☐ r ☐
10. 38 ÷ 7 = ☐ r ☐

11. 50 ÷ 4 = ☐ r ☐
12. 85 ÷ 6 = ☐ r ☐
13. 49 ÷ 3 = ☐ r ☐
14. 68 ÷ 5 = ☐ r ☐
15. 94 ÷ 4 = ☐ r ☐

16. There are 35 marbles. How many will be left over if they are shared equally between:
    a) 2 children
    b) 3 children
    c) 4 children
    d) 5 children?

C

Copy and complete.

1. ☐ ÷ 6 = 6 r 2
2. ☐ ÷ 7 = 6 r 2
3. ☐ ÷ 8 = 8 r 2
4. ☐ ÷ 9 = 9 r 2
5. ☐ ÷ 6 = 8 r 3

6. 69 ÷ ☐ = 9 r 6
7. 73 ÷ ☐ = 9 r 1
8. 80 ÷ ☐ = 8 r 8
9. 19 ÷ ☐ = 3 r 1
10. 38 ÷ ☐ = 5 r 3

11. 125 ÷ 4 = ☐ r ☐
12. 110 ÷ 6 = ☐ r ☐
13. 188 ÷ 5 = ☐ r ☐
14. 170 ÷ 8 = ☐ r ☐
15. 160 ÷ 3 = ☐ r ☐

16. What is the largest remainder you can have if you divide by:
    a) 3   b) 8   c) 100?

17. 24 25 30 51 75 80
    Which of the above numbers will have a remainder if divided by:
    a) 2   b) 3   c) 5?

I can decide whether to round up or down after division.

Examples

A relay team needs 4 runners.
There are 22 runners.
How many teams can be made?
22 ÷ 4 = 5 remainder 2
Answer: *5 teams can be made.*

4 children sit at each table.
There are 22 children.
How many tables are needed?
22 ÷ 4 = 5 remainder 2
Answer: *6 tables are needed.*

A

1. Two children can sit at each table. There are 17 children. How many tables are needed?

2. There are 28 children at a football club. How many 5-a-side teams can be made?

3. Ten children can sit on a bench. There are 68 children. How many benches are needed?

4. There are 15 children at a tennis club. How many pairs of children can be made?

5. David has 24 fish. He keeps no more than 10 fish in each tank. How many tanks does he need?

B

1. There are 6 huskies in each team. How many teams can be made from 40 huskies?

2. Zoe has 108 pens. Each packet holds 10 pens. How many packets does she need?

3. Derek can saw 3 boards from each plank. How many planks are needed to saw 25 boards?

4. There are 30 children in a P.E. lesson. How many teams of four can be made?

5. There are 27 children in a class. Six children can sit at each table. How many tables are needed?

C

1. 230 children are going on a trip. Each coach can carry 50 children. How many coaches are needed?

2. Rolls are sold in packets of 8. A baker has 46 rolls. How many packets can he make?

3. The 190 pupils in a school need a Maths exercise book. The books are sold in packs of 20. How many packs are needed?

4. A farmer has 46 eggs. A box holds 6 eggs. How many boxes can be filled?

5. 210 tickets have been sold for a school concert. 25 chairs make one row. How many rows of chairs are needed?

6. 40 children want to play netball. Each team has 7 players. How many teams can be made?

I can find pairs of numbers that total 100 and use them in calculations.

Examples

$100 - 58$ $\quad$ Answer 42 $\qquad$ $112 - 58$ $\quad$ Answer 54

A

1. $9 + 6$
2. $6 + 7$
3. $5 + 9$
4. $8 + 4$
5. $7 + 9$
6. $12 + 6$
7. $8 + 7$
8. $9 + 9$
9. $11 + 8$
10. $7 + 6$
11. $6 + 9$
12. $9 + 8$
13. $15 - 8$
14. $12 - 6$
15. $16 - 11$
16. $14 - 9$
17. $20 - 12$
18. $13 - 7$
19. $17 - 8$
20. $19 - 13$
21. $16 - 9$
22. $13 - 5$
23. $18 - 9$
24. $14 - 7$

B

Write the answers only.

1. $70 + 80$
2. $90 + 40$
3. $80 + 90$
4. $60 + 80$
5. $90 + 70$
6. $80 + 50$
7. $130 - 90$
8. $150 - 60$
9. $200 - 110$
10. $160 - 70$
11. $140 - 60$
12. $170 - 90$

What needs to be added to each number to make 100?

13. 25
14. 65
15. 45
16. 95
17. 15
18. 75
19. 42
20. 89
21. 34
22. 71
23. 6
24. 57

Work out

25. $103 - 85$
26. $126 - 93$
27. $111 - 78$
28. $109 - 49$
29. $133 - 87$
30. $117 - 95$
31. $121 - 54$
32. $105 - 63$
33. $119 - 68$
34. $135 - 92$
35. $108 - 71$
36. $127 - 83$
37. $142 - 96$
38. $104 - 57$
39. $116 - 48$
40. $124 - 75$

C

What needs to be added to each number to make 1000?

1. 350
2. 850
3. 50
4. 550
5. 250
6. 650
7. 730
8. 180
9. 940
10. 460
11. 810
12. 530

Copy and complete.

13. $900 + \square = 1400$
14. $600 + \square = 1200$
15. $500 + \square = 1300$
16. $700 + \square = 1400$
17. $1600 - \square = 800$
18. $1300 - \square = 600$
19. $1500 - \square = 900$
20. $1900 - \square = 700$
21. $213 - \square = 84$
22. $235 - \square = 157$
23. $242 - \square = 76$
24. $207 - \square = 54$
25. $358 - \square = 291$
26. $221 - \square = 68$
27. $314 - \square = 249$
28. $306 - \square = 153$

I can use a range of vocabulary associated with multiplication and division.

A

1. What is 6 times 2?

2. Multiply 5 by 7.

3. What is 10 multiplied by 8?

4. What is 9 lots of 2?

5. Find 6 groups of 5.

6. What is 10 times as big as 4?

7. Share 18 by 2.

8. Divide 70 by 10.

9. What is 45 divided by 5?

10. How many 2s make 14?

11. Share 20 by 5.

12. Divide 20 by 2.

13. What is 50 divided by 10?

14. How many 5s make 35?

15. Joan is 8. Her mother is 5 times older. How old is Joan's mother?

B

1. What is the sixth multiple of:
   a) 2   b) 5?

2. Multiply 3 by 8.

3. What is 5 times 100?

4. What is 21 multiplied by 2?

5. Find 3 lots of 40.

6. Find the product of 7 and 3.

7. What is 9 times greater than 4?

8. Rosie has 6 pens. Luke has three times as many. How many pens does Luke have?

9. How many teams of 4 can be made from 32 children?

10. 90 cm of string is cut into 3 equal lengths. How long is each length?

11. Jo has 20 sweets. She gives one quarter to Sita. How many does Jo have left?

12. There are 24 children in a class. One in every three have fair hair. How many children have fair hair?

C

Look at the numbers in the box.

> 3 8 15 20 24

1. What is the third multiple of the largest number?

2. Multiply the middle number by the second largest.

3. Which number is five times greater than the smallest number?

4. Ten different products can be made using pairs of the five numbers. Can you find them all?

5. A pack of 8 cans of drink costs £6·00. How much does each can of drink cost?

6. A tray of plants holds 6 flowers. How many trays can be filled from 54 flowers?

There are 48 people on a bus. One in every three is a man. Three in every eight are women.

7. How many men are on the bus?

8. How many women are on the bus?

I can find doubles of multiples of 5 to 100 and of multiples of 50 to 500 and all the halves of those doubles.

Examples

Double 35	Double 350	Half of 90	Half of 900
$(30 \times 2) + (5 \times 2)$	$(300 \times 2) + (50 \times 2)$	$(80 \div 2) + (10 \div 2)$	$(800 \div 2) + (100 \div 2)$
$60 + 10$	$600 + 100$	$40 + 5$	$400 + 50$
70	700	45	450

A

Work out

1. 10×2
7. 30×2
2. 6×2
8. 90×2
3. 9×2
9. 70×2
4. 12×2
10. 40×2
5. 7×2
11. 80×2
6. 5×2
12. 60×2

Work out

13. $26 \div 2$
19. $40 \div 2$
14. $10 \div 2$
20. $160 \div 2$
15. $16 \div 2$
21. $100 \div 2$
16. $22 \div 2$
22. $60 \div 2$
17. $12 \div 2$
23. $140 \div 2$
18. $28 \div 2$
24. $180 \div 2$

25. Copy and complete by doubling.

$1 \times 10 = \boxed{}$
$2 \times 10 = \boxed{}$
$4 \times 10 = \boxed{}$
$8 \times 10 = \boxed{}$
$16 \times 10 = \boxed{}$

Find one quarter of these numbers by halving and halving again.

26. 16
28. 12
27. 40
29. 20

B

Double

1. 35
7. 95
2. 75
8. 65
3. 250
9. 150
4. 55
10. 25
5. 85
11. 45
6. 450
12. 350

Halve

13. 300
19. 700
14. 130
20. 150
15. 70
21. 90
16. 500
22. 50
17. 190
23. 170
18. 110
24. 900

25. Work out the 8 times table by doubling the 4 times table.

Find one quarter of each number by halving and halving again.

26. 60
30. 36
27. 24
31. 1000
28. 300
32. 28
29. 180
33. 140

C

Double

1. 19
7. 290
2. 34
8. 420
3. 48
9. 180
4. 67
10. 370
5. 83
11. 260
6. 56
12. 490

Halve

13. 46
19. 280
14. 32
20. 470
15. 78
21. 540
16. 84
22. 910
17. 56
23. 720
18. 92
24. 390

25. Work out the 16 times table by doubling the 8 times table.

Find one quarter of each number by halving and halving again.

26. 220
30. 640
27. 52
31. 5000
28. 720
32. 96
29. 88
33. 14

I can multiply one-digit numbers by multiples of 10 to solve problems.

Examples

$5 \times 30 = 5 \times 3 \times 10$
$ = 15 \times 10$
$ = 150$

Each sweet weighs 20 g.
What is the weight of
eight sweets?

$8 \times 20\,g = 8 \times 2 \times 10\,g$
$ = 16 \times 10\,g$
$ = 160\,g$

A

Work out

1. 2×30
7. 2×20
2. 4×40
8. 5×30
3. 3×20
9. 2×50
4. 5×50
10. 4×20
5. 3×40
11. 5×40
6. 4×50
12. 3×30

13. Debbie buys two drinks costing 40p each. How much does she pay?

14. One wind turbine has three arms. How many arms do fifty turbines have?

15. Five loaves of bread are each cut into 20 slices. How many slices are there altogether?

16. Amir swims four lengths of a pool. Each length is 30 metres. How far does he swim altogether?

B

Work out

1. 6×40
7. 7×20
2. 2×70
8. 4×60
3. 7×50
9. 2×90
4. 9×60
10. 4×80
5. 8×30
11. 6×30
6. 3×80
12. 7×60

13. There are nine coins in a pile. Each coin weighs 20 g. What is the total weight of the coins?

14. There are four year groups in a Junior School. Each year has 60 children. How many children are there in the school?

15. Vera works for five days. She earns £70 each day. How much does she earn altogether?

16. Every day for a week Sonny reads 40 pages. How many pages does he read altogether?

C

Work out

1. 6×70
7. 7×300
2. 8×60
8. 3×800
3. 7×90
9. 5×600
4. 9×80
10. 9×900
5. 7×60
11. 6×800
6. 8×70
12. 5×700

13. The six performances of a play are each watched by 600 people.
How many people see the play?

14. Laura buys eight ice creams for 90p each. How much does she pay?

15. Four bottles each hold 700 ml of juice.
How much juice is there altogether?

16. A family of five are flying to Australia.
One plane ticket costs £800.
How much will the five tickets cost altogether?

I can solve one-step and two-step word problems.

Example

In 15 minutes 300 people cross the river by train on the rail bridge. Twice as many cross the river by car on the road bridge. How many people cross the river altogether?

$300 \times 2 = 600$
$600 + 300 = 900$
Altogether 900 people cross the river.

A

1 There are 40 toys in a shop. 15 are sold on Monday. Nine more are sold on Tuesday. How many toys are left?

2 One butterfly seems to have four eyes. How many eyes would 20 butterflies seem to have?

3 20 children are asked to choose their favourite colour. 8 children choose blue. Half of the rest choose red. How many children choose a different colour?

4 Annie buys a cake for 50p and a drink for 30p. She pays with £1. How much change will she have?

B

1 A cyclist travels 25 km in one hour. How far does she travel in 3 hours?

2 Helen is 33 years old. Sally is 21 years older. How old is Sally?

3 Phillip buys three ice creams for 80p each. He pays £5. How much change will he receive?

4 The Number 10 bus stops at a bus stop every 20 minutes. How many times does it stop there in six hours?

5 Jamie buys three packets of 8 Christmas cards and a box of 25 cards. How many cards has he bought?

6 Louise has one metre of wood. She saws off 40 cm. She saws off one quarter of the rest. What are the three lengths of wood she now has?

C

1 How many days are there in six weeks?

2 Sarah's book has 58 pages. She needs to read 5 more pages to reach half way. What page is she on?

3 A swimming pool is 25 metres long and 15 metres wide. Sharina swims six lengths and four widths. How far does she swim altogether?

4 Susan's book has 140 pages. She has finished page 50. She reads 15 pages every day. How long will it take her to finish the book?

5 There are 124 passengers on a train. 59 get off. At the next stop 23 more people get off. How many passengers are left on the train?

6 A can of cat food costs 40p. Oliver buys a pack of six cans for £1·85. How much has he saved by buying the pack?

I can solve mathematical problems or puzzles and investigate general statements.

Example
Find a pair of numbers with a sum of 25 and a product of 100.

Answer   *20 and 5*
20 + 5 = 25   20 × 5 = 100

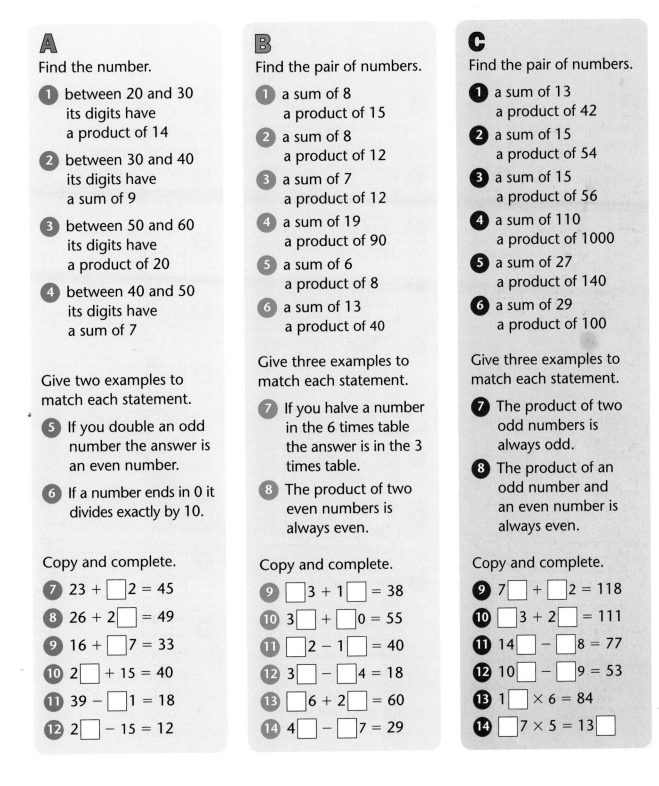

A

Find the number.

1. between 20 and 30
   its digits have
   a product of 14

2. between 30 and 40
   its digits have
   a sum of 9

3. between 50 and 60
   its digits have
   a product of 20

4. between 40 and 50
   its digits have
   a sum of 7

Give two examples to match each statement.

5. If you double an odd number the answer is an even number.

6. If a number ends in 0 it divides exactly by 10.

Copy and complete.

7. 23 + ☐2 = 45

8. 26 + 2☐ = 49

9. 16 + ☐7 = 33

10. 2☐ + 15 = 40

11. 39 − ☐1 = 18

12. 2☐ − 15 = 12

B

Find the pair of numbers.

1. a sum of 8
   a product of 15

2. a sum of 8
   a product of 12

3. a sum of 7
   a product of 12

4. a sum of 19
   a product of 90

5. a sum of 6
   a product of 8

6. a sum of 13
   a product of 40

Give three examples to match each statement.

7. If you halve a number in the 6 times table the answer is in the 3 times table.

8. The product of two even numbers is always even.

Copy and complete.

9. ☐3 + 1☐ = 38

10. 3☐ + ☐0 = 55

11. ☐2 − 1☐ = 40

12. 3☐ − ☐4 = 18

13. ☐6 + 2☐ = 60

14. 4☐ − ☐7 = 29

C

Find the pair of numbers.

1. a sum of 13
   a product of 42

2. a sum of 15
   a product of 54

3. a sum of 15
   a product of 56

4. a sum of 110
   a product of 1000

5. a sum of 27
   a product of 140

6. a sum of 29
   a product of 100

Give three examples to match each statement.

7. The product of two odd numbers is always odd.

8. The product of an odd number and an even number is always even.

Copy and complete.

9. 7☐ + ☐2 = 118

10. ☐3 + 2☐ = 111

11. 14☐ − ☐8 = 77

12. 10☐ − ☐9 = 53

13. 1☐ × 6 = 84

14. ☐7 × 5 = 13☐

I can use my understanding of division to find fractions of shapes and equivalent fractions.

Examples

10 equal parts

$\frac{7}{10}$ is shaded

10 equal parts

$\frac{2}{10}$ or $\frac{1}{5}$ is shaded

Write the fraction shaded as two equivalent fractions.

Answer $\frac{6}{8} = \frac{3}{4}$

$\left(\begin{array}{l} 6 \div 2 = 3 \\ \overline{8 \div 2 = 4} \end{array} \right)$

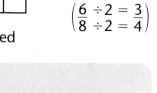

A

Write the fraction of each shape which is shaded.

1

5

2

6

3

7

4

8

Copy and complete by writing $\frac{1}{2}$ or $\frac{1}{4}$ in the box.

9 $\quad \frac{4}{8} = \square$

10 $\quad \frac{2}{8} = \square$

11 $\quad \frac{3}{12} = \square$

12 $\quad \frac{6}{12} = \square$

13 Find six different ways of shading one half of this square.

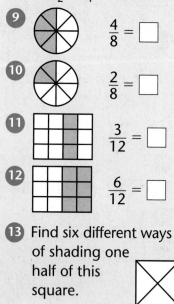

B

Copy and complete the equivalent fractions.

1 $\quad \frac{4}{8} = \frac{1}{\square}$

2 $\quad \frac{2}{10} = \frac{1}{\square}$

3 $\quad \frac{4}{12} = \frac{1}{\square}$

4 $\quad \frac{6}{8} = \frac{3}{\square}$

Write the fraction shown in two different ways.

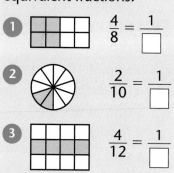

5

7

6

8

9 This is one way of shading one third of a strip of 6 squares.

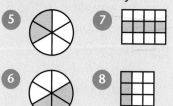

There are 15 different ways altogether. Can you find them all?

C

Copy and complete the equivalent fractions.

1 $\quad \frac{4}{6} = \frac{\square}{3}$

2 $\quad \frac{9}{12} = \frac{3}{\square}$

3 $\quad \frac{6}{10} = \frac{\square}{5}$

4 $\quad \frac{10}{12} = \frac{5}{\square}$

Write the fraction shown in two different ways.

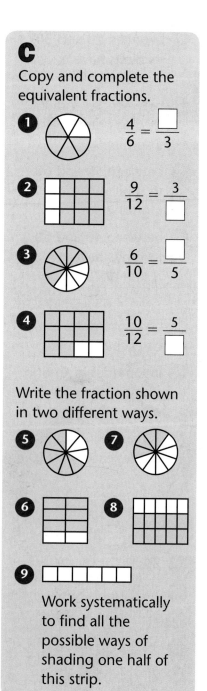

5

7

6

8

9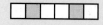

Work systematically to find all the possible ways of shading one half of this strip.

I can recognise whether an angle in a shape is a right angle, greater than a right angle or smaller than a right angle.

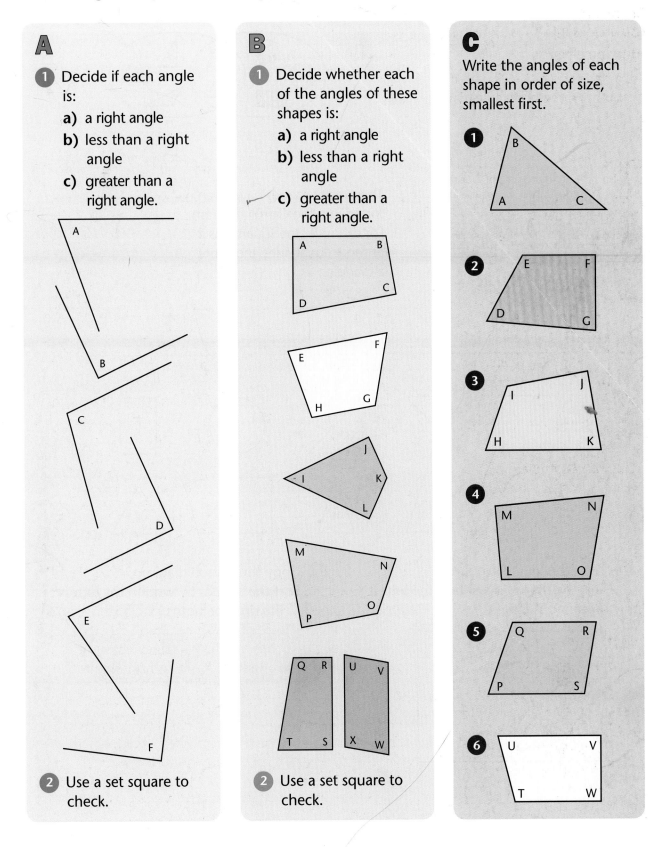

A

1 Decide if each angle is:

a) a right angle

b) less than a right angle

c) greater than a right angle.

2 Use a set square to check.

B

1 Decide whether each of the angles of these shapes is:

a) a right angle

b) less than a right angle

c) greater than a right angle.

2 Use a set square to check.

C

Write the angles of each shape in order of size, smallest first.

I can use Carroll diagrams or Venn diagrams to sort numbers or shapes.

Examples

This Venn diagram has been used to sort shapes into those which are:

a) symmetrical

b) a triangle

c) both symmetrical and a triangle.

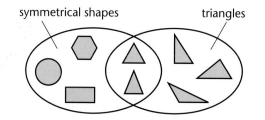

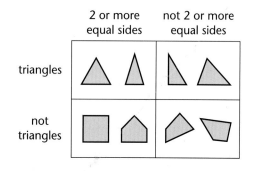

These eight shapes have been sorted into the Carroll diagram. For example, the square has 2 or more equal sides and is not a triangle.

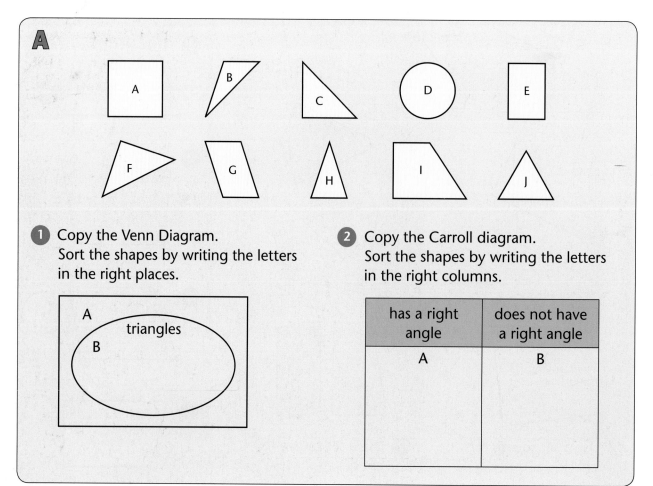

A

1 Copy the Venn Diagram.
Sort the shapes by writing the letters in the right places.

2 Copy the Carroll diagram.
Sort the shapes by writing the letters in the right columns.

has a right angle	does not have a right angle
A	B

B

1. Copy the Venn diagram. Sort the shapes by writing the letters in the right places.

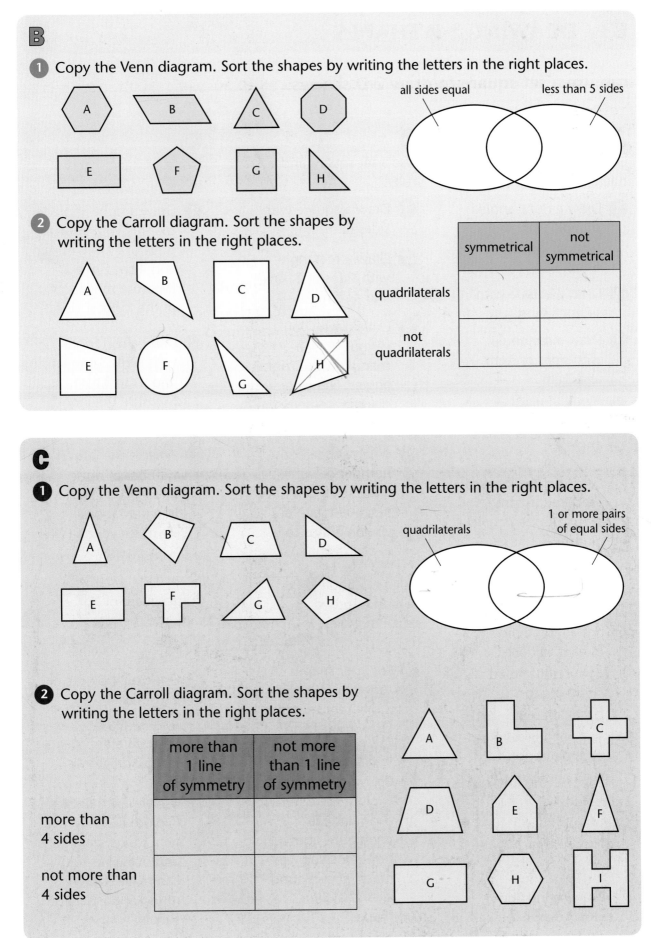

2. Copy the Carroll diagram. Sort the shapes by writing the letters in the right places.

	symmetrical	not symmetrical
quadrilaterals		
not quadrilaterals		

C

1. Copy the Venn diagram. Sort the shapes by writing the letters in the right places.

2. Copy the Carroll diagram. Sort the shapes by writing the letters in the right places.

	more than 1 line of symmetry	not more than 1 line of symmetry
more than 4 sides		
not more than 4 sides		

I can use a set square to draw 2-D shapes.

A

Use a set square and a ruler.

1. Draw a right-angled triangle with shorter sides of 2 cm and 6 cm.

2. Draw a square with sides of 4 cm.

3. Draw a rectangle with sides of 5 cm and 3 cm.

4. Can you draw a triangle with 2 right angles?

5. Use 2 squares of card that are the same size. Cut one in half along a diagonal.

6. Use all three pieces of card to make:
   a) a right-angled triangle
   b) 2 different quadrilaterals
   c) a pentagon
   d) a hexagon

   Example
   a pentagon

7. Draw round and label your shapes.

B

Use a set square and a ruler.

1. Draw a square with sides of $3\frac{1}{2}$ cm.

2. Draw a rectangle with sides of $2\frac{1}{2}$ cm and $4\frac{1}{2}$ cm.

3. Explain why you cannot draw a triangle with 2 right angles. Draw a diagram to help you explain this clearly.

4. What is the largest number of right angles you can have in a quadrilateral? Use diagrams to explain your answer.

Cut a rectangle of card into two equal triangles.

5. Put your shapes together to make 2 different triangles. Draw round and label your shapes.

6. Use your 2 triangles. Explore the different quadrilaterals, pentagons and hexagons you can make. Draw round and label your shapes.

C

Use a set square and a ruler.

1. Draw a right-angled triangle with shorter sides of 5 cm 6 mm and 4 cm 2 mm. Measure the length of the longest side.

2. Draw a rectangle with sides 3 cm 4 mm and 4 cm 8 mm. Measure the length of the diagonal.

3. What is the largest number of right angles you can have in a pentagon? Illustrate your answer with diagrams.

Cut a square of card into 4 equal triangles.

4. Using all 4 pieces of card make:
   a) a triangle
   b) 4 different quadrilaterals.

5. Use your 4 triangles. Explore the different pentagons, hexagons and octagons you can make. Draw round and label your shapes.

I can compare the data shown in two pictograms.

A

This pictogram shows how children in Class 3 came to school in January.

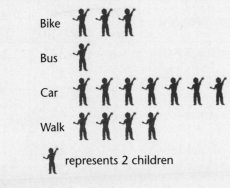

represents 2 children

1. Which was the most common way of getting to school?
2. Which was the least common?
3. How many children walked to school?
4. How many cycled?
5. How many more children came by car than walked?
6. How many fewer children came by bus than by bike?

B

This pictogram shows how children in Class 3 came to school in May.

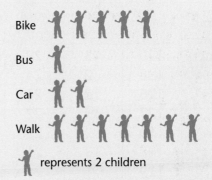

represents 2 children

Look at the pictograms in A and B.

1. How many children were in the class:
   a) in January   **b)** in May?
2. How many fewer children went to school by car in May than in January?
3. How many more children cycled in May than in January?
4. Can you suggest a reason for these changes?

C

1. How many children were in the Year 7 class?

Compare the data in this pictogram with that in Section B.

2. How many more Y7 than Y3 pupils went to school by:
   a) bike   **b)** bus   **c)** car?
3. How many fewer Y7 pupils walked?
4. Can you suggest reasons for these differences?

This pictogram shows how children in a Year 7 class travelled to their Secondary School in May.

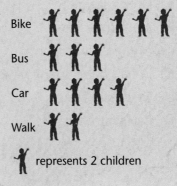

represents 2 children

I can compare data in two tables.

12 children recorded their height, shoe size, foot length and hand span in the Autumn Term and eight months later in the Summer Term. These are the results. (Height, foot length and hand span are shown in centimetres.)

AUTUMN TERM

Name	Height	Shoe size	Foot length	Hand span
Ahmed	120	13	22	15
Beth	138	2	24	17
Colin	116	12	21	16
Dee	127	13	22	15
Elton	130	2	23	17
Fiona	118	13	21	16
Gill	129	1	24	17
Henry	120	1	22	16
India	134	1	23	17
Joel	125	2	23	17
Kay	115	1	22	15
Leo	131	3	24	17

SUMMER TERM

Name	Height	Shoe size	Foot length	Hand span
Ahmed	124	1	23	15
Beth	141	2	25	18
Colin	118	13	22	16
Dee	133	1	23	17
Elton	134	4	24	18
Fiona	119	13	21	17
Gill	132	1	25	17
Henry	122	2	22	17
India	139	2	24	17
Joel	128	2	23	18
Kay	119	2	23	15
Leo	133	3	25	17

A

1. Who was the tallest in autumn?

2. Who was the shortest in summer?

3. How many children wore size 2 shoes:
   a) in autumn
   b) in summer?

4. Had these measurements gone up, gone down or stayed the same?
   a) Elton's height
   b) Joel's shoe size
   c) Ahmed's foot length
   d) India's hand span
   e) Dee's shoe size
   f) Kay's hand span

5. How much taller were these children in the summer than in the autumn?
   a) Colin   c) Leo
   b) Gill   d) Beth

6. Copy the Carroll diagram. Write the 12 names in the right places.

Shoe Size Bigger	Shoe Size Not Bigger

B

1. How many children had a foot length of over 23 cm:
   a) in autumn
   b) in summer?

2. How many children had a greater hand span in the summer than in the autumn?

3. Which children had the same hand span?

4. Whose height increased more?
   a) Colin or Kay
   b) Dee or India?

5. Which children had longer feet in the summer but wore the same size shoes?

6. Which child wore a larger shoe size in the summer but had the same foot length?

7. Copy the Venn diagram. Write the 12 names in the right places.

girls — more than 2 cm taller

8. Copy the Carroll diagram. Write the names in the right places.

	handspan bigger	handspan not bigger
boys		
not boys		

C

1. What was the difference in height between the tallest and the shortest child in:
   a) autumn
   b) summer?

2. Who had grown the most in height in the 8 months between the recording of the measurements?

3. Whose hand span had increased the most?

4. Whose foot length had increased the most?

5. Whose shoe size had increased the most?

6. Which children had the same hand span but had grown taller?

7. Copy the Venn diagram. Write the 12 names in the right places.

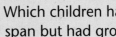

height below 130 cm in autumn — height above 130 cm in autumn

8. Copy the Carroll diagram. Write the names in the right places.

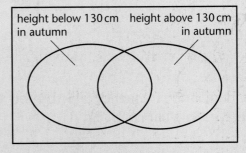

	more than 2 cm taller	not more than 2 cm taller
shoe size increased		
shoe size not increased		

I can make a tally chart and draw and use a bar chart.

Example

The ages of children in a basketball club.

10	9	8	10	9	10	11
8	10	11	9	10	8	10
9	10	10	8	11	10	9
10	11	9	10	8	9	10

A tally chart showing the ages.

Age	Tally	Total
8	卌	5
9	卌 ‖	7
10	卌 卌 ‖	12
11	‖‖	4

A frequency table showing the ages.

Ages	No. of children
8	5
9	7
10	12
11	4

The data in the frequency table can be displayed in a bar chart.

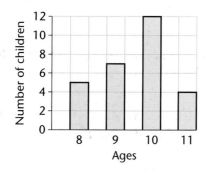

A

1. Class 3 were asked to choose their favourite lesson. The frequency table shows the results.

Subject	Votes
English	5
Maths	7
P.E.	8
Art	6

Draw a block graph to show the results.

This block graph shows the ages of children at a party.

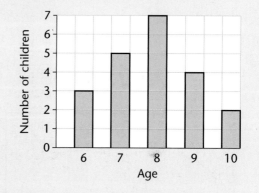

2. How many children were 7 years old?

3. What was the most common age?

4. How old was the youngest child at the party?

5. How many more children were 8 than 7?

6. How many children were over 8?

7. How many children were at the party altogether?

B

1. The members of a football club voted for the colour of their new kit. They chose from red, blue, gold and white. These are the results of the vote.

```
G  B  G  R  W  G  B  R
R  W  R  G  G  B  R  G
G  R  G  B  R  W  G  R
B  G  W  R  G  R  B  G
```

Make a tally chart and then draw a bar chart to show the results.

Class 3 put 20 seeds into 5 dishes. They put them in different places in the school grounds. One week later they counted the shoots in each dish. These are the results.

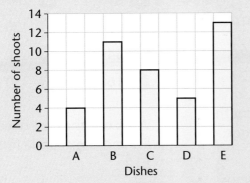

2. How many seeds had started to grow in Dish D?

3. In which dish had 8 seeds germinated?

4. How many dishes:

   a) had more than 10 shoots

   b) had less than 10 shoots?

5. How many more shoots were there in:

   a) Dish B than Dish C

   b) Dish E than Dish D?

6. How many fewer seeds had germinated in Dish A than Dish E?

C

1. The children in Year 3 were asked how they came to school. It was found that they walked or came by car, bus or train. These are the results.

```
C  B  W  C  T  W  C  C
C  W  C  B  W  C  T  W
B  C  T  C  W  W  B  C
C  C  W  C  B  C  W
C  W  B  C  T  C  W  C
```

Make a tally chart and then draw a bar chart to show the results.

The children in a school voted for the P.E. equipment they would like to be bought with a £100 prize. These are the results.

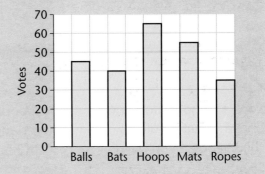

2. Which equipment got more than 50 votes?

3. Which equipment got less than 50 votes?

4. How many more children voted for balls than for bats?

5. How many fewer children voted for ropes than for mats?

6. Laura said that exactly one half of the votes were for either hoops or mats. Was she right? Explain your answer.

I can find change to solve money problems.

Example
What is the change from £5·00
for items costing £1·57?

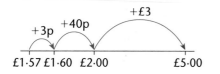

Answer   *£3·43*

SCHOOL SHOP PRICES

pencil	12p	sharpener	25p
pen	55p	notebook	28p
ruler	35p	calculator	£1·75
crayons	49p	T shirt	£3·20
rubber	19p	PE bag	£2·50

A

What needs to be added
to make 100?

1 80   **5** 10

2 25   **6** 55

3 70   **7** 60

4 45   **8** 35

Look at school shop prices
above. What would be
the change if you buy:

9 a sharpener for £1

10 a pen for £1

11 a ruler for £1

12 a calculator for £2

13 a T shirt for £5

14 a PE bag for £5?

15 How many rulers
could you buy for £1.
How much change
would you receive?

16 How many rubbers
could you buy for
£1? How much
change would you
receive?

B

What needs to be added
to each number to make
100?

1 46   **5** 52

2 93   **6** 19

3 38   **7** 67

4 71   **8** 24

Work out the cost of these
items and the change
from £5.

9 2 packs of crayons

10 T shirt, rubber

11 2 pens, pencil

12 calculator, notebook

13 I buy a pen and one
other item for £1.
I receive 33p change.
What is the other item?

14 I buy a sharpener and
one other item for £1.
I receive 47p change.
What is the other item?

15 How many T shirts can
be bought for £10?
How much change
would there be?

C

What needs to be added
to each number to make
1000?

1 830   **5** 780

2 270   **6** 420

3 540   **7** 610

4 160   **8** 350

Work out the cost of each
list and the change from
£10.

9 pencil   sharpener
crayons   PE bag

10 notebook   rubber
calculator   pen

11 I buy 2 T shirts, a
calculator and one
other item for £10.
I receive £1·57
change. What is the
other item?

12 I buy a PE bag,
5 pencils and one
other item for £10.
I receive £6·41
change. What is the
other item?

I can use doubling and halving to solve calculations.

Examples

Find the 8 times table by doubling the 4s.

FOURS	EIGHTS
4	8
8	16
12	24

and so on

Work out multiples of 15 by doubling.

$1 \times 15 = 15$
$2 \times 15 = 30$
$4 \times 15 = 60$
$8 \times 15 = 120$
$16 \times 15 = 240$

Find quarters and eighths of numbers by halving.

$\frac{1}{2}$ of $280 = 140$
$\frac{1}{4}$ of $280 = 70$
$\frac{1}{8}$ of $280 = 35$

A

1 Copy and complete by doubling.

$1 \times 20 = \boxed{}$
$2 \times 20 = \boxed{}$
$4 \times 20 = \boxed{}$
$8 \times 20 = \boxed{}$
$16 \times 20 = \boxed{}$

2 Find the 6 times table by doubling the 3s.

THREES	SIXES
3	6
6	12
9	18

and so on to ×10

Copy and complete by halving.

3 $\frac{1}{2}$ of $24 = \boxed{}$

$\frac{1}{4}$ of $24 = \boxed{}$

$\frac{1}{8}$ of $24 = \boxed{}$

4 $\frac{1}{2}$ of $80 = \boxed{}$

$\frac{1}{4}$ of $80 = \boxed{}$

$\frac{1}{8}$ of $80 = \boxed{}$

B

1 Copy and complete by doubling.

$1 \times 75 = \boxed{}$
$2 \times 75 = \boxed{}$
$4 \times 75 = \boxed{}$
$8 \times 75 = \boxed{}$
$16 \times 75 = \boxed{}$

2 Find the 12 times table by doubling the 6s.

3 Use halving to find one eighth of:
   a) 400 ml
   b) 32p
   c) £2.

4 COCONUT BISCUITS

   250 g flour
   60 g sugar
   100 g coconut
   2 eggs
   Makes 20 biscuits.

   Write out the recipe for:
   a) 40 biscuits
   b) 10 biscuits.

C

1 Work out multiples of 13 to 16×13 by doubling.

2 Use your multiples of 13 to find:
   a) 9×13
   b) 24×13
   c) 14×13.

3 Find the 16 times tables by doubling the 8s.

4 Use halving to find one eighth of:
   a) 360 g
   b) 96p
   c) 1000 ml.

5 CHOCOLATE SHAKE

   600 ml milk
   160 ml cream
   6 teaspoons of cocoa
   4 teaspoons of sugar
   Makes 4 milkshakes.

   Write out the recipe for:
   a) 8 chocolate shakes
   b) 1 chocolate shake.

I can solve word problems involving multiplication or division and can decide whether to round a remainder up or down.

Example

Dictionaries are 4 cm wide.
How many dictionaries can be
stored on a 90 cm shelf?

$90 \div 4 = 80 \div 4 + 10 \div 4$
$= 20 + 2\,r\,2$
$= 22\,r\,2$

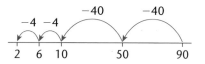

Answer   *22 dictionaries can be stored.*   (The remainder is rounded down.)

A

1 A bucket holds 5 litres of water. It takes 14 full buckets to fill a paddling pool. What is the capacity of the paddling pool?

2 A ribbon is 90 cm long. It is cut in half. How long are the two lengths?

3 There are 10 sweets in a packet. Each sweet weighs 15 g. How much do the sweets weigh altogether?

4 Sophie walks the same distance every day. In 5 days she walks 40 km. How far does she walk each day?

5 One lollipop costs 10p. Jack has 24p. How many lollipops can he buy?

B

1 One crate weighs 50 kg. What do three crates weigh?

2 Four biscuits weigh 100 g altogether? What does each biscuit weigh?

3 One tile is 16 cm long. What is the length of a row of six tiles?

4 One can of paint holds 3 litres. How many cans can be filled from 65 litres?

5 One bar of chocolate costs 40p. How much do four bars cost?

6 Each bag holds 6 kg of sand. How many bags are needed for 100 kg of sand?

7 Oranges cost 15p each. How many can be bought for £1?

C

1 How many complete weeks are there in 150 days?

2 A pizza weighs 240 g. It is cut into five slices. What does each slice weigh?

3 There are eight doses of medicine in a bottle. Each dose is 15 ml. How much medicine is in the bottle?

4 One train ticket costs £48. What do four tickets cost?

5 How many 15 cm lengths of wire can be cut from 2 metres?

6 Chloe saves £5 every week. How long will it take her to save the £126 she needs for her new bike?

7 How many complete minutes are there in 1000 seconds?

I can use rounding to approximate answers.

Examples

APPROXIMATE BY ROUNDING TO:

THE NEAREST 10	$38 + 52 \rightarrow 40 + 50 \rightarrow 90$
THE NEAREST 100	$480 - 290 \rightarrow 500 - 300 \rightarrow 200$
THE NEAREST POUND	$£2 \cdot 75 \times 6 \rightarrow £3 \times 6 \rightarrow £18$

A

Approximate

1. $38 + 14$
2. $29 + 28$
3. $42 + 21$
4. $33 + 35$

5. $47 - 16$
6. $63 - 34$
7. $51 - 28$
8. $89 - 42$

9. $£12 \cdot 40 + £9 \cdot 50$
10. $£8 \cdot 70 + £7 \cdot 10$
11. $£24 \cdot 60 - £16 \cdot 90$
12. $£15 \cdot 20 - £3 \cdot 80$

Approximate before solving.

13. Milly's father is 46. Her grandfather is 32 years older. How old is Milly's grandfather?
14. There are 58 people on a bus. 25 are upstairs. How many people are downstairs?
15. Mrs Brown spends £4·30 at the bakers and £7·60 at the butchers. How much does she spend altogether?

B

Approximate

1. $63 + 39$
2. $98 + 22$
3. $154 - 43$
4. $117 - 35$

5. $290 + 420$
6. $350 + 540$
7. $930 - 610$
8. $880 - 370$

9. $£3 \cdot 70 \times 4$
10. $£6 \cdot 40 \times 5$
11. $£7 \cdot 52 \times 3$
12. $£14 \cdot 91 \times 2$

Approximate before solving.

13. Jim has £127 in his savings account. He takes out £42. How much is left in the account?
14. One book costs £4·25. Gemma buys three books. How much does she spend?
15. Calvin has 79 British stamps and 38 foreign stamps. How many stamps does he have altogether?

C

Approximate

1. $87 + 64$
2. $223 + 59$
3. $165 - 76$
4. $108 - 51$

5. 790×4
6. 432×6
7. $860 \div 3$
8. $476 \div 10$

9. $£25 \cdot 35 \times 4$
10. $£39 \cdot 72 \times 6$
11. $£3 \cdot 70 \div 8$
12. $£7 \cdot 84 \div 10$

Approximate before solving.

13. There are 207 children in a school. 98 are girls. How many are boys?
14. A small can of dog food weighs 382 g. A large can weighs 228 g more. What does a large can weigh?
15. One cinema ticket costs £6·80. What do 8 tickets cost?

I can solve problems involving measures with mixed units.

Example

A pizza weighs half a kilogram.

It is cut into 10 equal slices.

How much does each slice weigh?

$\frac{1}{2}$ kg = 500 g

500 ÷ 10 = 50 g

Each slice weighs 50 g.

A

1. A tile weighs 40 g. What is the weight of 10 tiles?

2. A bottle of shampoo holds 200 ml. 80 ml is used. How much shampoo is now in the bottle?

3. A fence is 24 m long. Half of the fence has been painted. How long is the unpainted fence?

4. Alex weighs 38 kg. His brother weighs 13 kg more. How much does Alex's brother weigh?

5. A shower uses 7 litres of water in one minute. How much water is used in five minutes?

6. A block of flats is 40 m tall. A tree is 15 m shorter. How tall is the tree?

B

1. A pipe is 2 m long. 80 cm is cut off. How long is the pipe which is left?

2. A carton of cream contains 500 ml. How much cream is needed to fill 10 cartons? Give your answer in litres.

3. A cake weighs one kilogram. It is cut into five equal slices. How much does each slice weigh?

4. A man walks one and a half kilometres. He walks a further 400 m. How far has he walked altogether in metres?

5. A container of milk holds 2 litres. 500 ml is used. How much is left?

6. One tin of peas weighs 300 g. What do 8 tins weigh? Give your answer in kilograms and grams.

C

1. A parcel weighs one and a half kilograms. A second parcel weighs 800 g more. What is the combined weight of the parcels?

2. Eight glasses can be filled from a bottle of cola. Each glass holds 250 ml. How much cola is in the bottle in litres?

3. Harry's mother is one and a half metres tall. Harry is 27 cm shorter. How tall is Harry?

4. Twenty cans of beans weigh 8 kg altogether. What does one can weigh?

5. There is half a litre of water in a bowl. 600 ml of hot water and a quarter of a litre of cold is added. How much water is now in the bowl?

6. An athlete trains by running 800 metres five times. How far does she run in kilometres?

I can solve time problems by finding a time difference or by finding a start or end time.

Examples

A lesson starts at 9:40.

It lasts 50 minutes.

When does it finish?

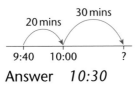

Answer *10:30*

A lesson lasts 40 minutes.

It finishes at 11:15.

When does it start?

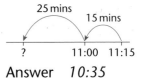

Answer *10:35*

A

1. Tina falls asleep at 8:05. She wakes up at 8:50. How long has she been asleep?

2. Playtime starts at 1:55. The bell is rung at 2:10. How long does afternoon play last?

3. Jack begins his painting at 2:35. He finishes it at 3:15. How long does the painting take?

4. Cora gets on the bus at 11:45. She gets off at 12:10. How long is her journey?

5. Nicky leaves for school at 7:55. He gets there at 8:30. How long does it take him to get to school?

6. Penny arrives at the station at 4:50. Her train leaves at 5:05. How long does she have to wait?

B

1. Lunchtime lasts 50 minutes. It finishes at 1:05. When does it start?

2. A rounders game starts at 1:30. It lasts 45 minutes. When does it finish?

3. A TV programme lasts 40 minutes. It starts at 6:45. When does it finish?

4. Drama Club lasts 55 minutes. It ends at 4:15. When does it begin?

5. Gerry puts a meal in the microwave oven at 4:55. It takes 25 minutes to cook. When is it ready to eat?

6. The boys took 35 minutes to reach the island. They arrived there at 11:10. When did they set off?

C

1. A chicken will take 1 hour 40 minutes to cook. It needs to be ready at 1:50. When should it go in the oven?

2. A plane takes off at 10:15. The flight lasts 1 hour 35 minutes. When does the plane land?

3. It starts to rain at 8:10. It stops at 10:05. How long has it been raining?

4. The play lasts 1 hour and 15 minutes. It must finish at 3:05. When should it start?

5. A tennis match starts at 3:20 and finishes at 4:45. How long does it last?

6. A Science lesson starts at 9:25. It lasts 70 minutes. When does it finish?

I can read scales to the nearest division or half-division.

Work out the measurement shown by each arrow.

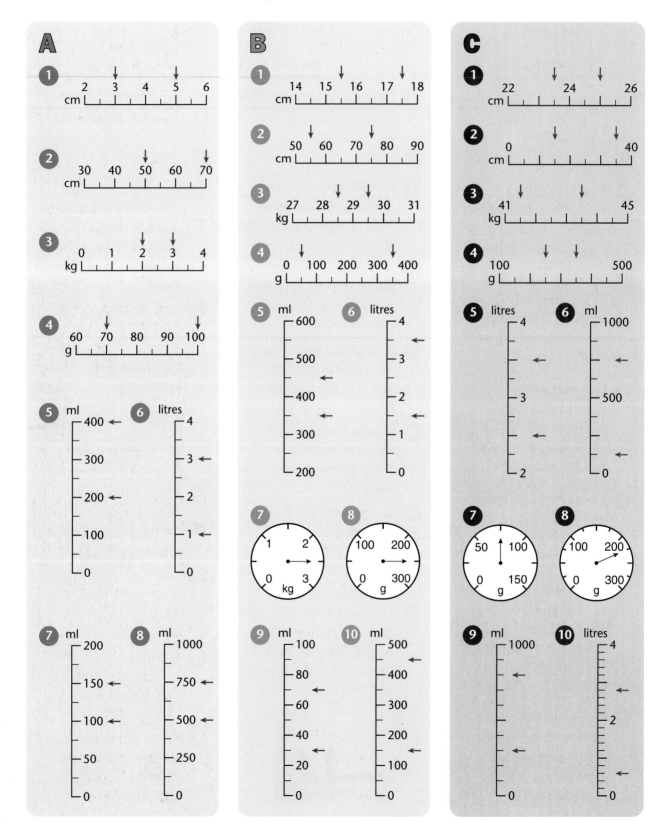

I can use a set square to compare angles with a right angle.

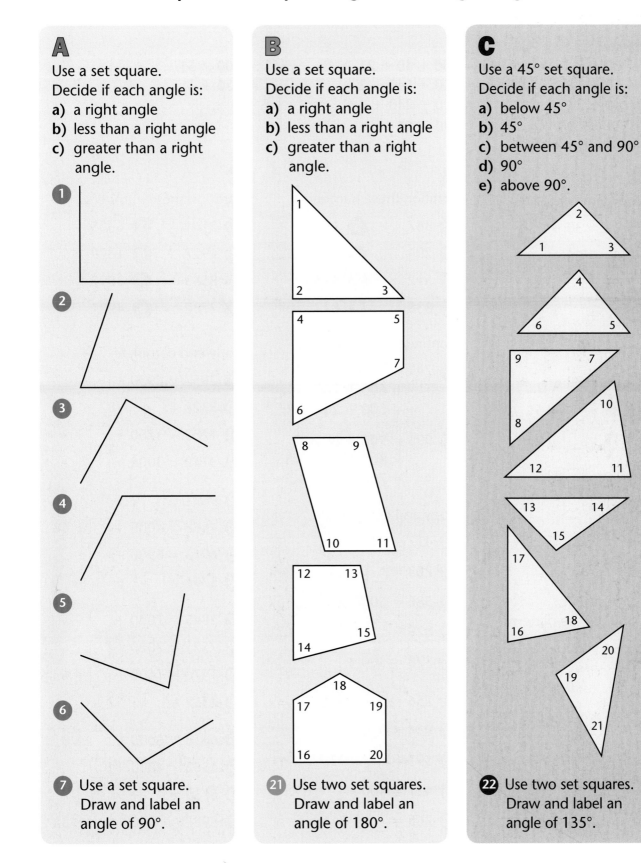

A

Use a set square.
Decide if each angle is:
a) a right angle
b) less than a right angle
c) greater than a right angle.

1

2

3

4

5

6

7 Use a set square.
Draw and label an angle of 90°.

B

Use a set square.
Decide if each angle is:
a) a right angle
b) less than a right angle
c) greater than a right angle.

21 Use two set squares.
Draw and label an angle of 180°.

C

Use a 45° set square.
Decide if each angle is:
a) below 45°
b) 45°
c) between 45° and 90°
d) 90°
e) above 90°.

22 Use two set squares.
Draw and label an angle of 135°.

I can partition numbers in different ways.

Numbers can be partitioned in different ways.

Examples

$67 = 60 + 7$
$\quad = 50 + 17$
$\quad = 40 + 27$
$\quad\quad$ and so on

$942 = 900 + 40 + 2$
$\quad\ = 800 + 140 + 2$
$\quad\ = 700 + 240 + 2$
$\quad\quad$ and so on

$351 = 300 + 51$
$\quad\ = 350 + 1$

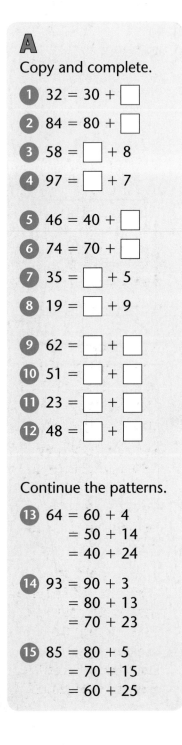

A

Copy and complete.

1. $32 = 30 + \boxed{}$

2. $84 = 80 + \boxed{}$

3. $58 = \boxed{} + 8$

4. $97 = \boxed{} + 7$

5. $46 = 40 + \boxed{}$

6. $74 = 70 + \boxed{}$

7. $35 = \boxed{} + 5$

8. $19 = \boxed{} + 9$

9. $62 = \boxed{} + \boxed{}$

10. $51 = \boxed{} + \boxed{}$

11. $23 = \boxed{} + \boxed{}$

12. $48 = \boxed{} + \boxed{}$

Continue the patterns.

13. $64 = 60 + 4$
$\quad\ = 50 + 14$
$\quad\ = 40 + 24$

14. $93 = 90 + 3$
$\quad\ = 80 + 13$
$\quad\ = 70 + 23$

15. $85 = 80 + 5$
$\quad\ = 70 + 15$
$\quad\ = 60 + 25$

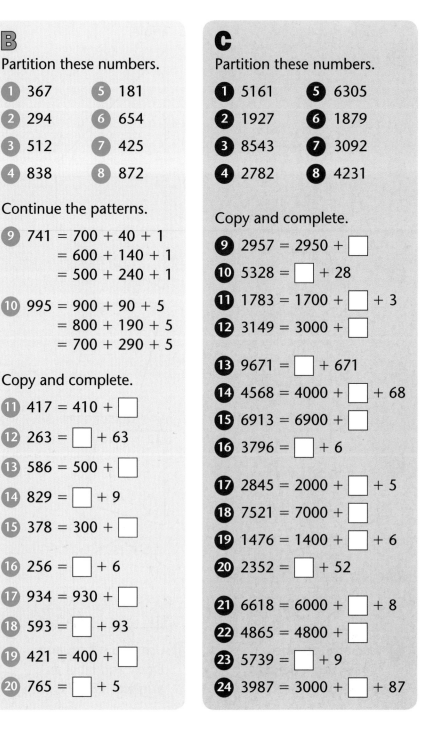

B

Partition these numbers.

1. 367
2. 294
3. 512
4. 838
5. 181
6. 654
7. 425
8. 872

Continue the patterns.

9. $741 = 700 + 40 + 1$
$\quad\ = 600 + 140 + 1$
$\quad\ = 500 + 240 + 1$

10. $995 = 900 + 90 + 5$
$\quad\ = 800 + 190 + 5$
$\quad\ = 700 + 290 + 5$

Copy and complete.

11. $417 = 410 + \boxed{}$

12. $263 = \boxed{} + 63$

13. $586 = 500 + \boxed{}$

14. $829 = \boxed{} + 9$

15. $378 = 300 + \boxed{}$

16. $256 = \boxed{} + 6$

17. $934 = 930 + \boxed{}$

18. $593 = \boxed{} + 93$

19. $421 = 400 + \boxed{}$

20. $765 = \boxed{} + 5$

C

Partition these numbers.

1. 5161
2. 1927
3. 8543
4. 2782
5. 6305
6. 1879
7. 3092
8. 4231

Copy and complete.

9. $2957 = 2950 + \boxed{}$

10. $5328 = \boxed{} + 28$

11. $1783 = 1700 + \boxed{} + 3$

12. $3149 = 3000 + \boxed{}$

13. $9671 = \boxed{} + 671$

14. $4568 = 4000 + \boxed{} + 68$

15. $6913 = 6900 + \boxed{}$

16. $3796 = \boxed{} + 6$

17. $2845 = 2000 + \boxed{} + 5$

18. $7521 = 7000 + \boxed{}$

19. $1476 = 1400 + \boxed{} + 6$

20. $2352 = \boxed{} + 52$

21. $6618 = 6000 + \boxed{} + 8$

22. $4865 = 4800 + \boxed{}$

23. $5739 = \boxed{} + 9$

24. $3987 = 3000 + \boxed{} + 87$

I can use a written method for addition calculations.

Examples

66 + 58

$$66 = 60 + 6$$
$$+ \underline{58} = \underline{50 + 8}$$
$$110 + 14 = 124$$

$$174 = 100 + 70 + 4$$
$$+ \underline{156} = \underline{100 + 50 + 6}$$
$$200 + 120 + 10 = 330$$

A

Copy and complete.

1. 23
    +24

2. 49
    +35

3. 37
    +22

4. 51
    +46

5. 44
    +26

6. 65
    +29

7. 72
    +36

8. 59
    +34

9. 66
    +37

10. 48
    +34

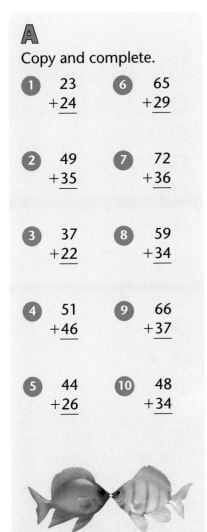

11. David has 34 blue fish and 57 gold fish. How many fish does he have altogether?

12. Maddy has 49 story books and 27 non-fiction books. How many books does she have altogether?

B

Copy and complete.

1. 62
    +47

2. 76
    +88

3. 98
    +73

4. 81
    +45

5. 54
    +59

6. 83
    +59

7. 67
    +74

8. 59
    +97

9. 75
    +38

10. 96
    +64

11. A shop sells 88 adult bikes and 83 children's bikes. How many bikes are sold altogether?

12. Carl has 65p in his piggy bank. He puts in another 47p. How much has he saved altogether?

C

Set out as in the example.

1. 116 + 147
2. 195 + 176
3. 262 + 135
4. 328 + 194
5. 353 + 287
6. 489 + 198
7. 534 + 283
8. 471 + 259
9. 545 + 398
10. 467 + 348

11. Sanjay buys a computer for £475 and a printer for £189. How much does he spend altogether?

12. Larry drives his lorry 259 miles on Monday and 293 miles on Tuesday. How far has he driven in the two days?

13. The School Concert is seen by 177 people in the afternoon and 184 people in the evening. How many people see the Concert altogether?

I can use a written method for subtraction calculations.

Examples

94 − 36

$$94 = 90 + 4 = 80 + 14$$
$$\underline{-36} = \underline{30 + 6} \quad \underline{30 + 6}$$
$$50 + 8 = 58$$

232 − 46

$$232 = 200 + 30 + 2 \qquad 100 + 120 + 12$$
$$\underline{- 46} \qquad\qquad \underline{40 + 6} \qquad \underline{40 + 6}$$
$$100 + 80 + 6 = 186$$

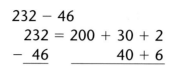

A

Copy and complete.

1 58
     −23

6 45
     −37

2 74
     −36

7 62
     −28

3 84
     −21

8 71
     −27

4 65
     −39

9 57
     −29

5 93
     −23

10 84
     −55

11 Billy's book has 91 pages. He has finished page 38. How many more pages does he have to read?

12 There are 75 children at the seaside. 48 are in the sea. How many are on the beach?

B

Copy and complete.

1 72
     −28

6 124
     − 62

2 85
     −38

7 181
     − 37

3 164
     − 39

8 225
     − 94

4 158
     − 97

9 163
     − 38

5 273
     − 45

10 156
     − 77

11 There are 142 people on board a boat. 59 get off. How many people are left on board?

12 A shop has 120 newspapers. 87 are sold. How many are not sold?

C

Set out as in the example.

1 282 − 136

2 229 − 145

3 376 − 168

4 561 − 232

5 604 − 273

6 453 − 195

7 315 − 266

8 740 − 398

9 630 − 485

10 827 − 569

11 Lynn earns £728. She spends £473. How much has she saved?

12 There are 364 people working in an office block. 246 are women. How many men work in the office block?

13 The school buys 520 exercise books. 231 are given out. How many are left in the stock cupboard?

I can make lists of multiplication facts to solve problems.

Example

Tara has 33 straws. She uses all the straws to make rectangles and pentagons. How many of each shape does she make?

Write out the 4 and 5 times tables to 33. Take one number from each list to make 33.

There are two possible solutions.
Tara makes 2 rectangles and 5 pentagons or 7 rectangles and 1 pentagon.

$1 \times 4 = 4$	$1 \times 5 = 5$
$2 \times 4 = 8$	$2 \times 5 = 10$
$3 \times 4 = 12$	$3 \times 5 = 15$
$4 \times 4 = 16$	$4 \times 5 = 20$
$5 \times 4 = 20$	$5 \times 5 = 25$
$6 \times 4 = 24$	$6 \times 5 = 30$
$7 \times 4 = 28$	
$8 \times 4 = 32$	

A

THE PROBLEM

A farmer keeps pigs and chickens. He counts 22 legs in his farmyard.
How many chickens does he see and how many pigs?
Find all the possible solutions.

METHOD

1 Write out the 2 times table to 22.

2 Write out the 4 times table to 20.

3 Take one number from each list to make 22.

4 Find the six possible solutions.

B

1 Screws are sold in packets of 3 or packets of 5. Derek buys 22 screws.
How many packets of 3 does he buy and how many packets of 5?

2 Small burgers cost £3. Large burgers cost £4. Lia buys burgers for £29.
How many large burgers does she buy and how many small burgers?
Find both possible solutions.

C

1 Ayub has 61 books. He sorts them into piles of 5 and piles of 9. There are no books left over. How many piles of 5 does he have and how many piles of 9?

2 Dolly the Dolphin is fed either 4 large fish or 7 small fish. Altogether she eats 50 fish. How many large fish does she eat and how many small fish? Find both possible solutions.

I can solve division problems, some involving sharing and some involving grouping.

Examples

There are 30 children in a class.
On a school trip they are shared
equally between six adult helpers.
How many children are with each adult?
30 ÷ 6 = 5
5 children are with each adult.

There are 32 children in a class.
On a school trip each adult will
look after a group of 4 children.
How many adults are needed?
32 ÷ 4 = 8
8 adults are needed.

A

1. Ruby has eighteen high heeled shoes. How many pairs does she have?

2. There are 15 cakes. They are divided equally between 5 plates. How many cakes are on each plate?

3. How many 10ps make 60p?

4. Two friends buy a 40p bar of chocolate to share between them. How much should they each pay?

5. A class of 30 children is sorted into teams of five. How many teams are there?

B

1. How many bags of four can be made from 28 oranges?

2. Mohammed has 18 straws. How many triangles can he make? How many hexagons? How many squares?

3. Two people share a prize of £24. How much does each win?

4. Four coins are the same. Altogether they make £2. What are the coins?

5. There are 42 children eating a school dinner. They sit at tables of six. How many tables are needed?

6. Ninety fish are divided equally into three tanks. How many fish are there in each tank?

C

1. One litre of lemonade is poured equally into five glasses. How much is in each glass?

2. How many hours make 300 minutes?

3. There are 128 books on a bookcase. They are divided equally between the four shelves. How many books are on each shelf?

4. Eight coins are the same. They make 40p. What are the coins?

5. How many 20ps are there in £5?

6. The 72 children in Year 3 voted for their favourite bird. One sixth chose the robin. How many children voted for the robin?

I can work out a remainder and decide whether to round up or down.

Examples

Tickets cost £5.
I have £34.
How many tickets can I buy?

34 ÷ 5 = 6 remainder 4.
Answer   *I can buy 6 tickets.*

A car can carry 5 people.
34 people need transport.
How many cars are needed?

34 ÷ 5 = 6 remainder 4.
Answer   *7 cars are needed.*

Do not write in this book

A

Copy and complete.

1. 17 ÷ 2 = 8 r ☐
2. 62 ÷ 10 = 6 r ☐
3. 38 ÷ 5 = ☐ r ☐
4. 13 ÷ 4 = ☐ r ☐

5. What is the biggest remainder you can have when you divide a number by 2?

6. There are 15 children at a tennis club. How many pairs of children can be made?

7. A baker makes 47 cakes. Five cakes can fit into one box. How many boxes are needed?

8. A florist has 93 flowers. There are ten flowers in every bunch. How many bunches can she make?

B

Work out

1. 25 ÷ 3
2. 26 ÷ 6
3. 29 ÷ 4
4. 23 ÷ 7
5. 19 ÷ 6
6. 33 ÷ 5
7. 34 ÷ 4
8. 21 ÷ 9

9. What is the biggest remainder you can have when you divide a number by:
   a) 3
   b) 4
   c) 5
   d) 6?

10. Cans of drink are sold in packs of four. There are 26 cans. How many packs of four can be made?

11. The 28 children in a class need rubbers. Each box holds 8 rubbers. How many boxes does the teacher need to collect?

12. Marcus has £20. Books cost £3 each. How many books can Marcus buy?

C

Work out

1. 24 ÷ 7
2. 50 ÷ 6
3. 78 ÷ 5
4. 49 ÷ 9
5. 40 ÷ 3
6. 38 ÷ 6
7. 59 ÷ 8
8. 42 ÷ 4

9. What is the biggest remainder you can have when you divide a number by 10? Give a reason for your answer.

10. There are 148 empty bottles. Each crate holds 20 bottles. How many crates are needed?

11. Kerry has £50. C.D.s cost £9 each. How many C.D.s can she buy?

I can multiply one-digit numbers by multiples of 10 to solve problems.

Examples

$5 \times 30 = 5 \times 3 \times 10$
$= 15 \times 10$
$= 150$

Lily has eight 20ps. How much does she have altogether?

$8 \times 20p = 8 \times 2 \times 10p$
$= 16 \times 10p$
$= 160p$ or £1·60

A

Work out

1. 3×30
2. 2×50
3. 5×40
4. 3×20
5. 4×50
6. 5×20
7. 2×30
8. 3×40
9. 2×20
10. 4×40
11. 5×30
12. 3×50

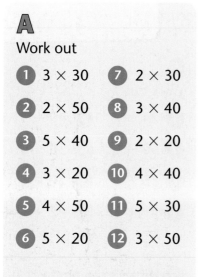

13. One brick is 20 cm long. How long is a row of four bricks?

14. Thomas has five 50ps. How much does he have altogether?

15. One train ticket costs £40. What do six tickets cost?

16. One page of an exercise book has 30 lines. Olivia writes four pages. How many lines has she written?

17. One sweet weighs 20 g. What do six sweets weigh?

B

Work out

1. 3×60
2. 6×20
3. 5×70
4. 9×50
5. 4×90
6. 7×30
7. 5×60
8. 8×40
9. 3×80
10. 9×20
11. 2×60
12. 6×50

13. One ice cream costs 90p. What do four ice creams cost?

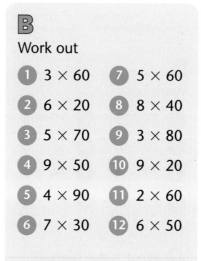

14. There are 30 exercise books in each packet. How many exercise books are there in six packets?

15. Josh makes the same 60 mile journey every day for a week. How far does he travel altogether?

16. A bookcase has eight shelves. There are 50 books on each shelf. How many books are on the bookcase?

C

Work out

1. 6×70
2. 9×60
3. 8×90
4. 6×80
5. 7×60
6. 9×70
7. 8×200
8. 6×300
9. 4×800
10. 6×600
11. 7×500
12. 5×900

13. A model of a bridge is 4 metres long. The actual bridge is 70 times longer. How long is the bridge?

14. One cake costs 80p. What do 5 cakes cost?

15. How many minutes are there in 8 hours?

16. Emily earns £500 each week. How much does she earn in six weeks?

17. A horse gallops 400 metres each minute. How far does he gallop in three minutes?

I can multiply two-digit numbers by one-digit numbers.

Example

16 × 4

10 × 4   6 × 4

0   40   64

16 × 4 = 10 × 4 plus 6 × 4
= 40 plus 24
= 64

×	10	6
4	40	24

40 + 24 = 64

A

Work out

1. 14 × 2
2. 12 × 5
3. 13 × 4
4. 25 × 3

5. 14 × 5
6. 28 × 2
7. 16 × 3
8. 17 × 4

9. Jessica has 23 pairs of socks. How many socks does she have altogether?

10. There are five rows of 16 chairs. How many chairs are there altogether?

11. Harry takes four pills each day for 12 days. How many pills does he take altogether?

12. Sophie buys three pencils for 14p each. How much does she pay?

B

Work out

1. 19 × 5
2. 27 × 3
3. 11 × 6
4. 18 × 4

5. 46 × 2
6. 14 × 6
7. 22 × 4
8. 18 × 3

9. 12 × 6
10. 16 × 4
11. 32 × 3
12. 17 × 5

13. 24 × 4
14. 15 × 6
15. 37 × 2
16. 29 × 3

17. A small packet has 18 pins. The largest packet has 5 times as many. How many pins are in the largest packet?

18. There are 21 tents at a camp site. There are four scouts to each tent. How many scouts are camping?

19. One ticket to enter a castle costs £3. How much will 25 tickets cost?

20. There are 6 eggs in each box. How many eggs are there in 13 boxes?

C

Work out

1. 19 × 6
2. 35 × 4
3. 28 × 5
4. 13 × 7

5. 95 × 2
6. 27 × 6
7. 56 × 3
8. 14 × 9

9. 67 × 3
10. 36 × 6
11. 48 × 4
12. 23 × 8

13. 28 × 6
14. 36 × 5
15. 79 × 2
16. 25 × 7

17. One length of a swimming pool is 22 metres. Charlie swims 9 lengths. How far does he swim?

18. Stamps cost 36p each. What do seven stamps cost?

19. There are 32 chess pieces in each set. How many pieces are there in eight sets?

20. Hard hats are stacked in sixes. There are 29 stacks at the building site. How many hats are there?

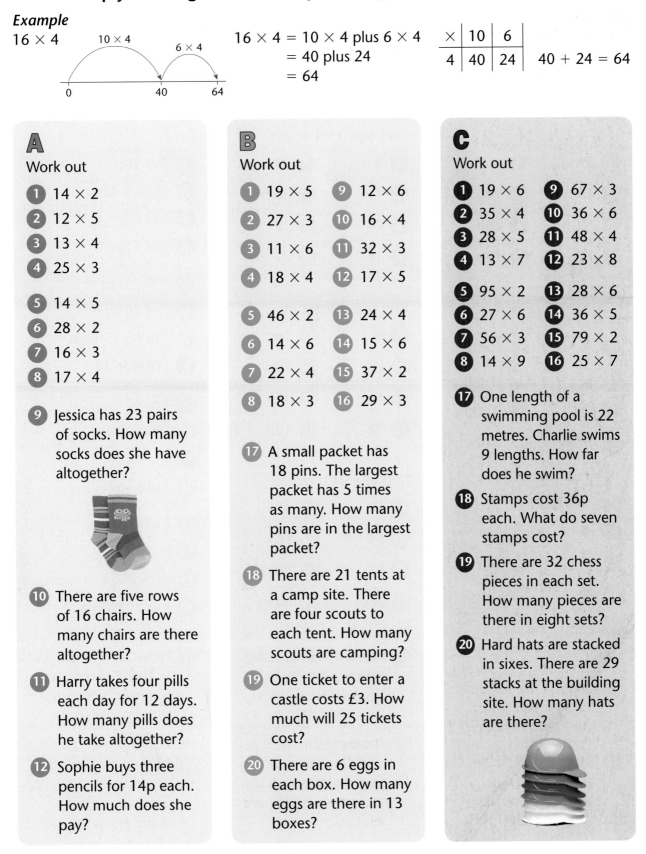

I can use multiplication facts to find fractions of numbers.

Examples

$\frac{1}{3}$ of 18 = 18 ÷ 3
= 6

$\frac{1}{5}$ of 40p = 40p ÷ 5
= 8p

$\frac{1}{4}$ of 120 g = 120 g ÷ 4
= 30 g

A

Find one half of:

1. 8
2. 16
3. 10
4. 12
5. 6p
6. 14p
7. 20p
8. 18p

Find one fifth of:

9. 25
10. 45
11. 10
12. 30
13. 40 cm
14. 50 cm
15. 15 cm
16. 35 cm

Find one tenth of:

17. 20
18. 80
19. 40
20. 100
21. 60p
22. 90p
23. 70p
24. 50p

25. Ian buys five sweets for 20p. How much does one sweet cost?

26. There are 30 grapes on a bunch. One tenth are eaten. How many are left?

B

Find one third of:

1. 9
2. 15
3. 24
4. 18
5. 21 cm
6. 30 cm
7. 12 cm
8. 27 cm

Find one quarter of:

9. 8
10. 28
11. 16
12. 32
13. 36p
14. 20p
15. 40p
16. 12p

Find one sixth of:

17. 30
18. 54
19. 12
20. 36
21. 42 kg
22. 18 kg
23. 60 kg
24. 24 kg

25. Fatma's mother is 48. Fatma is one sixth her age. How old is Fatma?

26. There are 24 chocolates in a box. One quarter are eaten. How many are left?

C

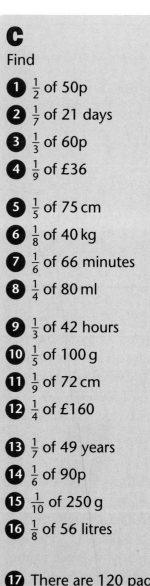

Find

1. $\frac{1}{2}$ of 50p
2. $\frac{1}{7}$ of 21 days
3. $\frac{1}{3}$ of 60p
4. $\frac{1}{9}$ of £36
5. $\frac{1}{5}$ of 75 cm
6. $\frac{1}{8}$ of 40 kg
7. $\frac{1}{6}$ of 66 minutes
8. $\frac{1}{4}$ of 80 ml
9. $\frac{1}{3}$ of 42 hours
10. $\frac{1}{5}$ of 100 g
11. $\frac{1}{9}$ of 72 cm
12. $\frac{1}{4}$ of £160
13. $\frac{1}{7}$ of 49 years
14. $\frac{1}{6}$ of 90p
15. $\frac{1}{10}$ of 250 g
16. $\frac{1}{8}$ of 56 litres

17. There are 120 pages in David's book. He has read one sixth. What page has he reached?

18. There are 32 children in a class. One eighth are absent. How many are at school?

I can read and write fractions.

Examples

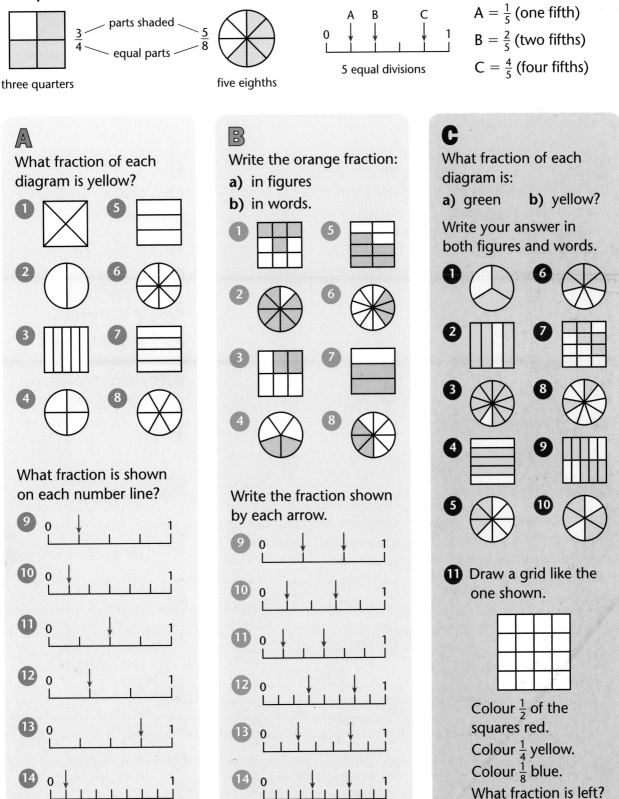

I can compare fractions and find pairs of fractions that make 1.

Examples

Pairs of fractions that look different but are the same are equivalent fractions.

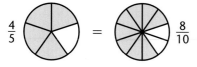

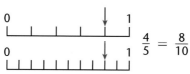

Some pairs of fractions make one whole one.

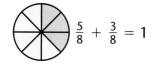

$\frac{5}{8} + \frac{3}{8} = 1$

A

Use the number lines to complete the equivalent fractions.

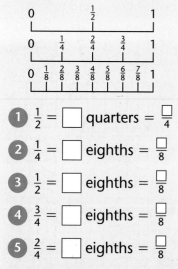

1 $\frac{1}{2} = \square$ quarters $= \frac{\square}{4}$

2 $\frac{1}{4} = \square$ eighths $= \frac{\square}{8}$

3 $\frac{1}{2} = \square$ eighths $= \frac{\square}{8}$

4 $\frac{3}{4} = \square$ eighths $= \frac{\square}{8}$

5 $\frac{2}{4} = \square$ eighths $= \frac{\square}{8}$

Use the diagram to complete the pair of fractions that make one whole one.

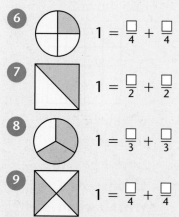

6 $1 = \frac{\square}{4} + \frac{\square}{4}$

7 $1 = \frac{\square}{2} + \frac{\square}{2}$

8 $1 = \frac{\square}{3} + \frac{\square}{3}$

9 $1 = \frac{\square}{4} + \frac{\square}{4}$

B

Use the number lines to complete the equivalent fractions.

1 $\frac{1}{3} = \frac{\square}{6}$ 5 $\frac{1}{3} = \frac{\square}{12}$

2 $\frac{4}{6} = \frac{\square}{12}$ 6 $\frac{3}{6} = \frac{\square}{12}$

3 $\frac{2}{3} = \frac{\square}{12}$ 7 $\frac{2}{3} = \frac{\square}{6}$

4 $\frac{1}{6} = \frac{\square}{12}$ 8 $\frac{5}{6} = \frac{\square}{12}$

Use the diagram to complete each pair of fractions that make one whole one.

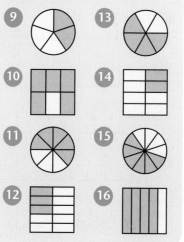

C

Copy and complete these fraction chains.

1 $\frac{1}{2} = \frac{\square}{4} = \frac{\square}{8} = \frac{\square}{16}$

2 $\frac{1}{2} = \frac{\square}{4} = \frac{\square}{6} = \frac{\square}{8}$

3 $\frac{1}{3} = \frac{\square}{6} = \frac{\square}{9} = \frac{\square}{12}$

4 $\frac{3}{4} = \frac{\square}{8} = \frac{\square}{12} = \frac{\square}{16}$

Which is the odd one out in each set of fractions?

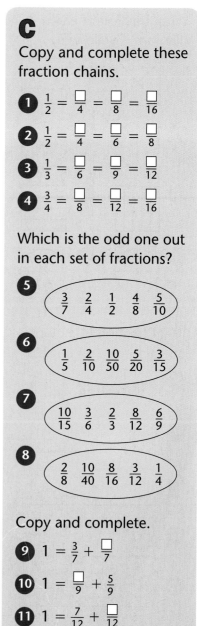

5 $\frac{3}{7} \quad \frac{2}{4} \quad \frac{1}{2} \quad \frac{4}{8} \quad \frac{5}{10}$

6 $\frac{1}{5} \quad \frac{2}{10} \quad \frac{10}{50} \quad \frac{5}{20} \quad \frac{3}{15}$

7 $\frac{10}{15} \quad \frac{3}{6} \quad \frac{2}{3} \quad \frac{8}{12} \quad \frac{6}{9}$

8 $\frac{2}{8} \quad \frac{10}{40} \quad \frac{8}{16} \quad \frac{3}{12} \quad \frac{1}{4}$

Copy and complete.

9 $1 = \frac{3}{7} + \frac{\square}{7}$

10 $1 = \frac{\square}{9} + \frac{5}{9}$

11 $1 = \frac{7}{12} + \frac{\square}{12}$

12 $1 = \frac{1}{8} + \frac{\square}{8}$

NUMBERS REVIEW

Write in words.

1. 57
2. 183
3. 340
4. 612
5. 725
6. 206
7. 494
8. 879

Give the value of the underlined digit.

9. 1_4_2
10. _6_38
11. 20_5_
12. 4_9_1
13. _7_26
14. 5_6_3
15. 91_7_
16. _3_89

Count on in 10s:

17. 50 from 136
18. 30 from 340
19. 60 from 508
20. 40 from 251.

Count back in 10s:

21. 40 from 273
22. 50 from 465
23. 70 from 592
24. 60 from 874.

Count on in 100s:

25. 300 from 634
26. 600 from 278
27. 500 from 122
28. 700 from 257.

Copy the sequence. Write the next three numbers.

29. 7   9   11   13
30. 25   22   19   16
31. 11   21   31   41
32. 35   30   25   20
33. 10   14   18   22
34. 25   28   31   34
35. 26   24   22   20
36. 12   17   22   27
37. 40   36   32   28
38. 50   100   150

Which number is smaller?

39. 213 or 231
40. 682 or 628
41. 735 or 753

Write in order. Start with largest.

42. 275   572   752   257
43. 894   948   849   489
44. 136   361   163   316

Round to the nearest:

10	100

45. 23
46. 57
47. 72
48. 45
49. 160
50. 340
51. 650
52. 874.

Estimate the numbers shown by the arrows.

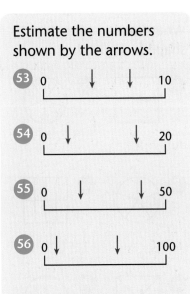

53. 0 ↓ ↓ 10
54. 0 ↓ ↓ 20
55. 0 ↓ ↓ 50
56. 0↓ ↓ 100

Write odd or even for each of these numbers.

57. 23
58. 16
59. 85
60. 14
61. 30
62. 49
63. 7
64. 72

Write the first four multiples of:

65. 3
66. 11
67. 20
68. 6.

30	28	21	20
27	15	50	35

Write the numbers in the box which are multiples of:

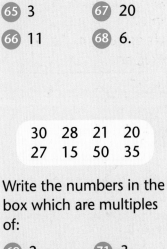

69. 2
70. 5
71. 3
72. 10.

FRACTIONS REVIEW

What fraction of each shape is shaded?

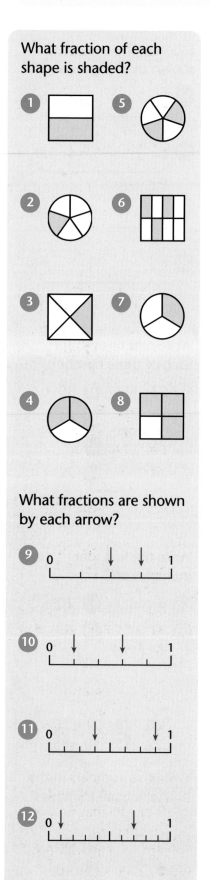

1

5

2

6

3

7

4

8

What fractions are shown by each arrow?

9   0 ↓ ↓ 1

10   0 ↓ ↓ 1

11   0 ↓ ↓ 1

12   0 ↓ ↓ 1

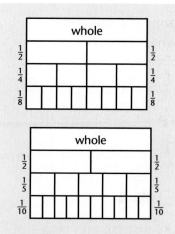

whole

$\frac{1}{2}$ $\frac{1}{2}$

$\frac{1}{4}$ $\frac{1}{4}$

$\frac{1}{8}$ $\frac{1}{8}$

whole

$\frac{1}{2}$ $\frac{1}{2}$

$\frac{1}{5}$ $\frac{1}{5}$

$\frac{1}{10}$ $\frac{1}{10}$

Use the fraction charts to copy and complete the equivalent fractions.

13   $1 = \dfrac{\Box}{5}$

14   $\dfrac{1}{4} = \dfrac{\Box}{8}$

15   $\dfrac{1}{2} = \dfrac{\Box}{10}$

16   $1 = \dfrac{\Box}{8}$

17   $\dfrac{3}{4} = \dfrac{\Box}{8}$

18   $\dfrac{1}{5} = \dfrac{\Box}{10}$

19   $\dfrac{1}{2} = \dfrac{\Box}{4}$

20   $1 = \dfrac{\Box}{10}$

21   $\dfrac{4}{5} = \dfrac{\Box}{10}$

22   $\dfrac{1}{2} = \dfrac{\Box}{8}$

Find one half of:

23   20

24   12

25   18

26   24

27   16

28   28

29   14

30   30.

Find one quarter of:

31   8 cm

32   28 cm

33   16 cm

34   20 cm

35   12 cm

36   40 cm

37   24 cm

38   32 cm.

Find one tenth of:

39   10p

40   £1

41   50p

42   20p

43   40p

44   70p

45   30p

46   90p.

47   There are 40 children born in a hospital. Half of them are boys. How many are girls?

48   There are 36 people in the sea. One quarter of them are surfing. How many people are surfing?

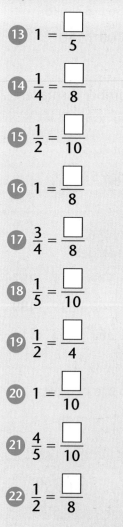

CALCULATIONS REVIEW

Work out.

1 35 + 17

2 46 + 300

3 1000 − 300

4 80 + 45

5 78 − 21

6 1200 − 500

7 100 − 55

8 68 − 32

9 1000 − 600

10 200 − 192

11 34 + 19

12 256 + 70

Copy and complete.

13 73
       +65

17 91
       −44

14 64
       +28

18 68
       −35

15 53
       +27

19 82
       −63

16 92
       +76

20 70
       −26

Copy and complete.

21

+	19	26	32
27			
30		56	
45			77

Double these numbers.

22 20

24 65

23 800

25 17

Halve these numbers.

26 140

28 700

27 36

29 190

Copy and complete.

30

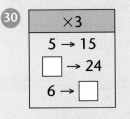

×3
5 → 15
☐ → 24
6 → ☐

31

×4
8 → ☐
☐ → 36
6 → ☐

Copy and complete.

32 7 × 4 = ☐

33 9 × 3 = ☐

34 5 × ☐ = 40

35 10 × ☐ = 60

36 ☐ = 8 × 8

37 ☐ = 3 × 21

38 16 ÷ 2 = ☐

39 45 ÷ 5 = ☐

40 30 ÷ ☐ = 5

41 7 ÷ ☐ = 1

42 ☐ ÷ 8 = 3

43 ☐ ÷ 4 = 5

Copy and complete by writing the remainder.

44 48 ÷ 5 = 9 r ☐

45 19 ÷ 3 = 6 r ☐

46 30 ÷ 4 = 7 r ☐

47 87 ÷ 10 = 8 r ☐

48 There are 28 children in 4W and 26 in 4H. How many children are there in both classes?

49 There are 32 chocolates in a box. Half of them are eaten. How many chocolates are left?

50 Lee's book has 80 pages. He finishes page 35. How many pages does he still have to read?

51 There are 4 tins in each pack. How many tins are there in 8 packs?

52 How many groups of 3 can be made from 26 children? How many children are left over?

MEASURES REVIEW

Make 1 metre.

1. 50 cm + ☐
2. 85 cm + ☐
3. 35 cm + ☐
4. 55 cm + ☐

Make 1 km.

5. 800 m + ☐
6. 100 m + ☐
7. 400 m + ☐
8. 700 m + ☐

Write as grams.

9. 3 kg 100 g
10. 2·5 kg

Write as litres.

11. 4000 ml
12. 7500 ml

Work out the measurement shown by each arrow.

13.
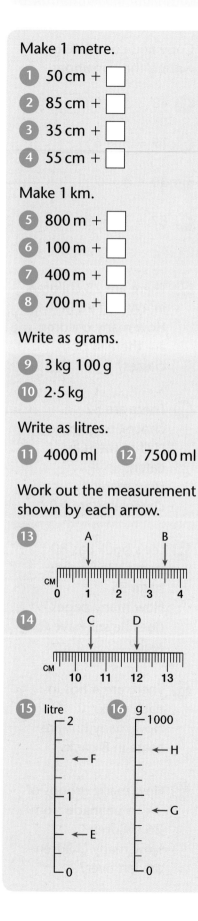

14.

15. litre
16. g

---

17. A piece of wood is 90 cm long. It is sawn in half. How long is each piece?

18. A bottle holds 800 ml of water. 300 ml is poured out. How much water is left?

19. A bag of potatoes weighs 5 kg. How much do 6 bags weigh?

20. Sam ran 38 km last week and 29 km this week. How far has he run altogether?

Write as minutes.

21. 30 seconds
22. 2 hours

Write as days.

23. 10 weeks
24. 48 hours

Write as weeks.

25. 1 year
26. 21 days

Write the times shown:
a) in words
b) in figures, using am and pm

27. afternoon
28. morning

29. 6:25 evening
30. 2:15 night

MARCH						
Su	M	Tu	W	Th	F	Sa
	1	2	3	4	5	6
7	8	9	10	11	12	13
14	15	16	17	18	19	20
21	22	23	24	25	26	27
28	29	30	31			

31. How many days are there in March?

32. How many Tuesdays are there in the month shown in the calendar?

33. On which day of the week does March 19th fall?

34. A lesson starts at 9:45. It lasts 35 minutes. At what time does the lesson finish?

SHAPE REVIEW

Write the names of each of these 2-D shapes.

1

2

3

4

Use squared paper.
Copy the shapes.
Draw on two lines of symmetry on each shape.

5 M

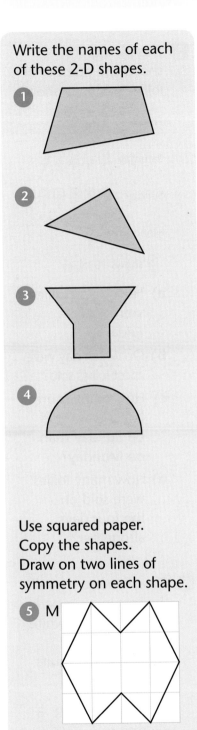

6 M

Write the names of each of these 3-D shapes.

7

8

9

10

How many cubes are needed to build each shape?

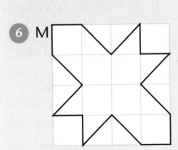

11

13

12

14

15 Give the position of all eight symbols.

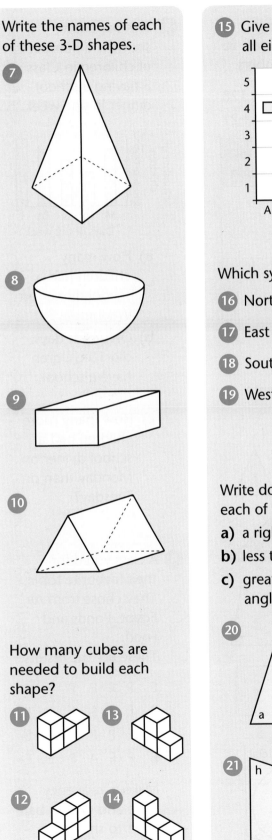

Which symbol is found.

16 North of ○

17 East of □

18 South of △

19 West of ●?

Write down whether each of the angles is:

a) a right angle

b) less than a right angle

c) greater than a right angle.

20

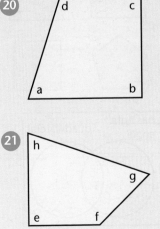

21

HANDLING DATA REVIEW

1 Copy the Carroll diagram and use it to sort these numbers.

34 115 12 7 128
4 63 149 10 21

	even	not even
two digits		
not two digits		

2 Copy the Venn diagram and write the letters in the correct places.

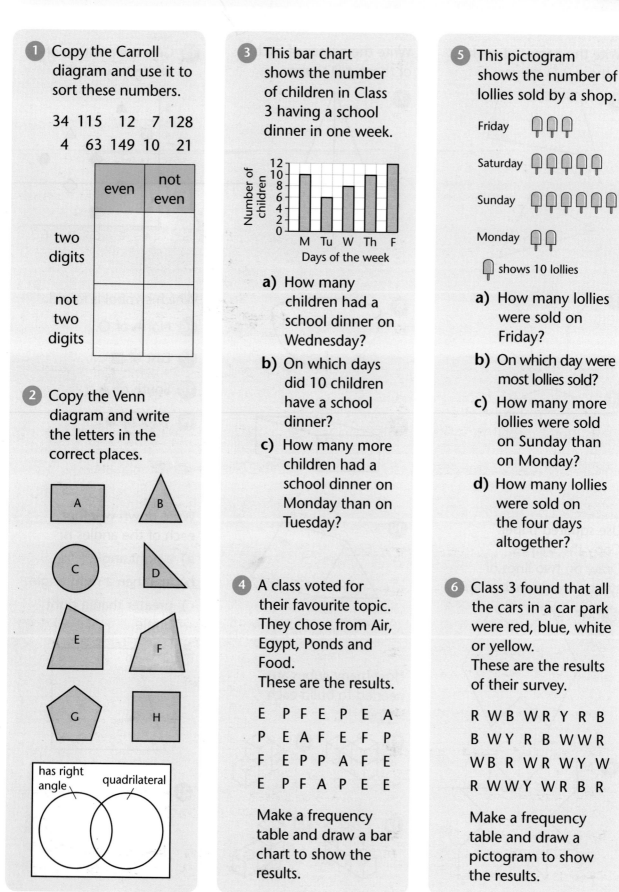

3 This bar chart shows the number of children in Class 3 having a school dinner in one week.

a) How many children had a school dinner on Wednesday?

b) On which days did 10 children have a school dinner?

c) How many more children had a school dinner on Monday than on Tuesday?

4 A class voted for their favourite topic. They chose from Air, Egypt, Ponds and Food.
These are the results.

E P F E P E A
P E A F E F P
F E P P A F E
E P F A P E E

Make a frequency table and draw a bar chart to show the results.

5 This pictogram shows the number of lollies sold by a shop.

Friday
Saturday
Sunday
Monday

shows 10 lollies

a) How many lollies were sold on Friday?

b) On which day were most lollies sold?

c) How many more lollies were sold on Sunday than on Monday?

d) How many lollies were sold on the four days altogether?

6 Class 3 found that all the cars in a car park were red, blue, white or yellow.
These are the results of their survey.

R W B W R Y R B
B W Y R B W W R
W B R W R W Y W
R W W Y W R B R

Make a frequency table and draw a pictogram to show the results.

TEST 1

1. Write two hundred and fifty-eight in figures.

2. Add 35 to 400.

3. Round 760 to the nearest 100.

4. What is 7 times 5?

5. Write 312 pence as pounds and pence.

6. Take 19 from 65.

7. How many metres make one kilometre?

8. Share 18 by 3.

9. A carton of milk contains one litre. 300 ml is used. How much milk is left?

10. What is 400 more than 230?

11. Double 45.

12. How many days are there in five weeks?

13. How many boxes of four can be made from 24 balls?

14. Holly has two pounds. She spends £1·40. How much has she left?

15. How many quarters make a whole one?

16. Write two and a half litres in millilitres.

17. What is 36 divided by 4?

18. Saheed has 77 marbles. Ryan has 43 marbles less than Saheed. How many marbles does Ryan have?

TEST 2

1. What is the difference between 65 and 100?

2. How many 50 pence pieces make £10?

3. What is seven multiplied by three?

4. Write five hundred and seven in figures.

5. What is the sum of 43 and 25?

6. What is one half of 700?

7. How many grams are there in one and a half kilograms?

8. A television programme starts at 8:10. It lasts 35 minutes. When does it finish?

9. What is 3 less than 400?

10. What is one tenth of 30 pence?

11. Round 68 to the nearest 10.

12. Find the product of 8 and 4.

13. What is 19 more than 27?

14. 25 centimetres is cut from one metre of wood. How much wood is left?

15. What is the cost of five pens at 30 pence each?

16. How many minutes are there in ten hours?

17. How many groups of three can be made from 24 children?

18. There are 58 children in a swimming pool. 21 are boys. How many are girls?

How to learn a times table.

BY YOURSELF

1. Read the table over and over.

2. Cover the table and say it out loud or in your mind.

3. Say it more and more quickly.

4. Try to say the table backwards.

WITH A FRIEND

Ask each other questions like:

What is 6 times 4?

Multiply 4 by 7.

How many fours make 32?

Divide 36 by 4.

$1 \times 1 = 1$	$1 \times 2 = 2$	$1 \times 3 = 3$	$1 \times 4 = 4$	$1 \times 5 = 5$
$2 \times 1 = 2$	$2 \times 2 = 4$	$2 \times 3 = 6$	$2 \times 4 = 8$	$2 \times 5 = 10$
$3 \times 1 = 3$	$3 \times 2 = 6$	$3 \times 3 = 9$	$3 \times 4 = 12$	$3 \times 5 = 15$
$4 \times 1 = 4$	$4 \times 2 = 8$	$4 \times 3 = 12$	$4 \times 4 = 16$	$4 \times 5 = 20$
$5 \times 1 = 5$	$5 \times 2 = 10$	$5 \times 3 = 15$	$5 \times 4 = 20$	$5 \times 5 = 25$
$6 \times 1 = 6$	$6 \times 2 = 12$	$6 \times 3 = 18$	$6 \times 4 = 24$	$6 \times 5 = 30$
$7 \times 1 = 7$	$7 \times 2 = 14$	$7 \times 3 = 21$	$7 \times 4 = 28$	$7 \times 5 = 35$
$8 \times 1 = 8$	$8 \times 2 = 16$	$8 \times 3 = 24$	$8 \times 4 = 32$	$8 \times 5 = 40$
$9 \times 1 = 9$	$9 \times 2 = 18$	$9 \times 3 = 27$	$9 \times 4 = 36$	$9 \times 5 = 45$
$10 \times 1 = 10$	$10 \times 2 = 20$	$10 \times 3 = 30$	$10 \times 4 = 40$	$10 \times 5 = 50$

$1 \times 6 = 6$	$1 \times 7 = 7$	$1 \times 8 = 8$	$1 \times 9 = 9$	$1 \times 10 = 10$
$2 \times 6 = 12$	$2 \times 7 = 14$	$2 \times 8 = 16$	$2 \times 9 = 18$	$2 \times 10 = 20$
$3 \times 6 = 18$	$3 \times 7 = 21$	$3 \times 8 = 24$	$3 \times 9 = 27$	$3 \times 10 = 30$
$4 \times 6 = 24$	$4 \times 7 = 28$	$4 \times 8 = 32$	$4 \times 9 = 36$	$4 \times 10 = 40$
$5 \times 6 = 30$	$5 \times 7 = 35$	$5 \times 8 = 40$	$5 \times 9 = 45$	$5 \times 10 = 50$
$6 \times 6 = 36$	$6 \times 7 = 42$	$6 \times 8 = 48$	$6 \times 9 = 54$	$6 \times 10 = 60$
$7 \times 6 = 42$	$7 \times 7 = 49$	$7 \times 8 = 56$	$7 \times 9 = 63$	$7 \times 10 = 70$
$8 \times 6 = 48$	$8 \times 7 = 56$	$8 \times 8 = 64$	$8 \times 9 = 72$	$8 \times 10 = 80$
$9 \times 6 = 54$	$9 \times 7 = 63$	$9 \times 8 = 72$	$9 \times 9 = 81$	$9 \times 10 = 90$
$10 \times 6 = 60$	$10 \times 7 = 70$	$10 \times 8 = 80$	$10 \times 9 = 90$	$10 \times 10 = 100$